An Analysis of

C. S. Lewis's

The Abolition of Man

Ruth Jackson
with
Brittany Pheiffer Noble

Published by Macat International Ltd
24:13 Coda Centre, 189 Munster Road, London SW6 6AW.

Distributed exclusively by Routledge
2 Park Square, Milton Park, Abingdon, Oxon OX14 4RN
711 Third Avenue, New York, NY 10017, USA

Routledge is an imprint of the Taylor & Francis Group, an informa business

Copyright © 2017 by Macat International Ltd
Macat International has asserted its right under the Copyright, Designs and Patents Act
1988 to be identified as the copyright holder of this work.

www.macat.com
info@macat.com

Cataloguing in Publication Data
A catalogue record for this book is available from the British Library.
Library of Congress Cataloguing-in-Publication Data is available upon request.
Cover illustration: Etienne Gilfillan

ISBN 978-1-912302-46-8 (hardback)
ISBN 978-1-912128-92-1 (paperback)
ISBN 978-1-912281-34-3 (e-book)

Notice
The information in this book is designed to orientate readers of the work under analysis,
to elucidate and contextualise its key ideas and themes, and to aid in the development
of critical thinking skills. It is not meant to be used, nor should it be used, as a
substitute for original thinking or in place of original writing or research. References and
notes are provided for informational purposes and their presence does not constitute
endorsement of the information or opinions therein. This book is presented solely for
educational purposes. It is sold on the understanding that the publisher is not engaged
to provide any scholarly advice. The publisher has made every effort to ensure that
this book is accurate and up-to-date, but makes no warranties or representations with
regard to the completeness or reliability of the information it contains. The information
and the opinions provided herein are not guaranteed or warranted to produce particular
results and may not be suitable for students of every ability. The publisher shall not be
liable for any loss, damage or disruption arising from any errors or omissions, or from
the use of this book, including, but not limited to, special, incidental, consequential or
other damages caused, or alleged to have been caused, directly or indirectly, by the

CONTENTS

THE MACAT LIBRARY

The Macat Library is a series of unique academic explorations of seminal works in the humanities and social sciences – books and papers that have had a significant and widely recognised impact on their disciplines. It has been created to serve as much more than just a summary of what lies between the covers of a great book. It illuminates and explores the influences on, ideas of, and impact of that book. Our goal is to offer a learning resource that encourages critical thinking and fosters a better, deeper understanding of important ideas.

Each publication is divided into three Sections: Influences, Ideas, and Impact. Each Section has four Modules. These explore every important facet of the work, and the responses to it.

This Section-Module structure makes a Macat Library book easy to use, but it has another important feature. Because each Macat book is written to the same format, it is possible (and encouraged!) to cross-reference multiple Macat books along the same lines of inquiry or research. This allows the reader to open up interesting interdisciplinary pathways.

To further aid your reading, lists of glossary terms and people mentioned are included at the end of this book (these are indicated by an asterisk [*] throughout) – as well as a list of works cited.

Macat has worked with the University of Cambridge to identify the elements of critical thinking and understand the ways in which six different skills combine to enable effective thinking.
Three allow us to fully understand a problem; three more give us the tools to solve it. Together, these six skills make up the **PACIER** model of critical thinking. They are:

ANALYSIS – understanding how an argument is built
EVALUATION – exploring the strengths and weaknesses of an argument
INTERPRETATION – understanding issues of meaning

CREATIVE THINKING – coming up with new ideas and fresh connections
PROBLEM-SOLVING – producing strong solutions
REASONING – creating strong arguments

To find out more, visit **WWW.MACAT.COM.**

CRITICAL THINKING AND *THE ABOLITION OF MAN*

Primary critical thinking skill: EVALUATION
Secondary critical thinking skill: REASONING

C.S. Lewis's 1943 *The Abolition of Man* is a set of three essays that encapsulate some of the most important elements of good critical thinking. Lewis considers a weighty topic, moral philosophy – and more precisely how we teach it, and where morality comes from. As critics and enthusiasts for Lewis's work alike have noted, though, he was not a philosopher as such, but a professor of literature. And rather than presenting novel or original ideas, the essays' true qualities lie in the ways in which they evaluate and judge the arguments of prior philosophers, and how they construct a coherent, highly persuasive argument for Lewis's own point of view.

Lewis takes issue with textbooks and philosophies that argue for (or imply) that all morals and moral judgments are relative. He deploys evaluative skills to point out the weaknesses in such arguments and then sets out for his readers the kind of moral future such relativism could lead to. This hard-hitting evaluation, in turn, provides a solid base upon which to construct a well-argued counter-proposal, that moral laws can be absolute, and stem from objective, universal values. Persuasive and enthralling, The Abolition of Man showcases reasoning at its best.

ABOUT THE AUTHOR OF THE ORIGINAL WORK

C. S. Lewis was born in Belfast, Northern Ireland, in 1898, and won a scholarship to University College, Oxford. World War I interrupted his education and he fought in the trenches of the Somme, but he eventually graduated in 1923 and worked as an academic at both Oxford and Cambridge.

Lewis had always been captivated by legend and mythology—a passion he shared with his friend and colleague, *The Lord of the Rings* author J. R. R. Tolkien. He went on to write many fiction and non-fiction books, including the famous Narnia series, all of them underpinned by a deep Christian faith. He died in 1963.

ABOUT THE AUTHORS OF THE ANALYSIS

Dr Ruth Jackson did postgraduate work in theology and religious studies at the University of Cambridge. She is currently acting Director of Studies at Corpus Christi College and is a researcher at the Centre for Research in the Arts, Social Sciences, and Humanities at Cambridge, where she works on the ERC-funded project 'The Bible and Antiquity in Nineteenth-Century Culture.'

Brittany Pheiffer Noble is a graduate student at Columbia University and holds a Masters degree from Yale University's Divinity School, where she studied religion and theology. Her research focuses on literary and aesthetic theory, alongside theology and history. She is the translator of Arab Orthodox Christians Under the Ottomans 1516–1831 (2016) and has taught at Sciences Po, Columbia and Dartmouth.

ABOUT MACAT

GREAT WORKS FOR CRITICAL THINKING

Macat is focused on making the ideas of the world's great thinkers accessible and comprehensible to everybody, everywhere, in ways that promote the development of enhanced critical thinking skills.

It works with leading academics from the world's top universities to produce new analyses that focus on the ideas and the impact of the most influential works ever written across a wide variety of academic disciplines. Each of the works that sit at the heart of its growing library is an enduring example of great thinking. But by setting them in context – and looking at the influences that shaped their authors, as well as the responses they provoked – Macat encourages readers to look at these classics and game-changers with fresh eyes. Readers learn to think, engage and challenge their ideas, rather than simply accepting them.

'Macat offers an amazing first-of-its-kind tool for interdisciplinary learning and research. Its focus on works that transformed their disciplines and its rigorous approach, drawing on the world's leading experts and educational institutions, opens up a world-class education to anyone.'

Andreas Schleicher
Director for Education and Skills, Organisation for Economic
Co-operation and Development

'Macat is taking on some of the major challenges in university education ... They have drawn together a strong team of active academics who are producing teaching materials that are novel in the breadth of their approach.'

Prof Lord Broers,
former Vice-Chancellor of the University of Cambridge

'The Macat vision is exceptionally exciting. It focuses upon new modes of learning which analyse and explain seminal texts which have profoundly influenced world thinking and so social and economic development. It promotes the kind of critical thinking which is essential for any society and economy. This is the learning of the future.'

Rt Hon Charles Clarke, former UK Secretary of State for Education

'The Macat analyses provide immediate access to the critical conversation surrounding the books that have shaped their respective discipline, which will make them an invaluable resource to all of those, students and teachers, working in the field.'

Professor William Tronzo, University of California at San Diego

WAYS IN TO THE TEXT

KEY POINTS

- C. S. Lewis (1898–1963) was a scholar and author. He is best known for his successful series of children's books *The Chronicles of Narnia*,* which were made into films after his death. He also wrote fiction for adults, essays, poetry, and a memoir, *Surprised by Joy*, as well as books defending Christian* belief.

- Written in 1943, *The Abolition of Man* reveals Lewis's unhappiness with British education and with how moral relativism* (that is, the idea that no set of moral beliefs is better than any other) has become rampant in modern society.

- The text is remarkable for its witty style, its explanation of various philosophical traditions, and its constant support for moral objectivism* (a system of ethics or values that has inherent truth and that can be followed by everyone whatever their time or culture and wherever they are from).

Who Was C. S. Lewis?

Clive Staples Lewis (1898–1963), the author of *The Abolition of Man* (1943), was born in Belfast, Northern Ireland, to a family of Protestant* Christians (one of the major forms of Christianity,* with its own doctrines and practices, of which the Anglican Church* forms a part). He had a difficult childhood; his mother died from cancer when he was just nine, and he spent his next years at four different schools before returning home to study with a private tutor. He also abandoned his faith at the age of 15. In 1916 Lewis, who asked friends and family to call him "Jack," won a scholarship to University College, Oxford. World War I* disrupted his education, however, and in 1917 and 1918 he fought in the trenches of the Somme* in France, one of the longest and bloodiest battles of the entire conflict.

In 1923 Lewis graduated from the University of Oxford with a first-class degree in English, Greek, and Latin literature, as well as classical literature and philosophy. He became a fellow* of Magdalen College in 1924, and remained in Oxford as a lecturer and tutor in English until 1954, when he obtained a position at Cambridge University.

As a teenager, Lewis was captivated by Icelandic mythology,* Norse sagas,* and ancient lyrical poetry.* He loved the poetry of Irishman W. B. Yeats* and old Irish history, and his private tutor, William T. Kirkpatrick, encouraged his interest in Classical Greek* literature. The young Lewis was also influenced by George MacDonald,* the writer of fantasy and fairy tales.

In 1931, inspired in part by his friendship with the devout Catholic J. R. R. Tolkien,* author of the influential works of fantasy *The Lord of the Rings*, Lewis converted back to Christianity, joining the Anglican Church. His charming and witty writing style has made Lewis's texts on Christianity, as well as his fiction, popular even in the twenty-first century.

Lewis spent his final years at the University of Cambridge, in the role of Professor of Medieval and Renaissance Literature. He died from renal failure at the age of 64, in 1963.

What Does *The Abolition of Man* Say?

In *The Abolition of Man*, Lewis argues against the idea that no set of beliefs is better than any other ("moral relativism") and also against the theory of emotivism* (the idea that ethical statements merely reflect emotional states). The text also criticizes the prevalent view of the time that put science center stage, insisting instead that irresponsible attitudes to technology will harm future generations. Lewis particularly dislikes the idea that schoolchildren are taught that values are subjective—that is, merely a matter of individual choice. Instead, he believes that if a society is going to flourish, people must accept that morality is not a matter of personal opinion, and that there is such a thing as a "moral law" that applies to everyone.

Lewis believes that there has been a decline in the quality of education because people have lost respect for "the doctrine of objective value." By this, he means a belief that some attitudes are really true, and others really false.

The book owes many of its principal themes, particularly its criticism of moral relativism, to Lewis's commitment to Anglican traditions (that is, the traditions of the Church of England). Before his re-conversion to Christianity in 1931, Lewis maintained a belief in a superhuman and eternal source of moral truth. This belief, dating from his adolescence, was based on his love of Classical Greek philosophy and, in particular, of the philosophers Plato* and Aristotle.*

As well as moral truth, Lewis places a high value on the importance of literature and beauty, as he makes clear in his discussion of art, poetry, and mythology. Modern education is wrong, he says, for dismissing beauty and wonder just because these "values" cannot be scientifically verified; the cost of living without them is a world without enchantment, in which we live in a disenchanted state.

For Lewis, morals and value judgments have a universal, unchanging, and objective source. He focuses on various traditions— Christianity, the Indian religion of Hinduism,* the Chinese notion of Tao* (according to which we are obliged to follow principles of action that accord morally with the natural order), and Ancient Greek philosophy—to show how they all point to a universal source for these morals and values.

If we do not understand this and instead see morals and values as relative, Lewis believes we resort to pragmatism* (where usefulness becomes the basis of value). This leads to disenchantment and exploitation—both of the natural world and of other people. Lewis is adamant that nature must not be reduced to something for humanity to make use of: "Now I take it that when we understand a thing analytically and then dominate and use it for our own convenience, we reduce it to the level of 'nature' in the sense that we suspend our judgments of value about it, ignore its final cause (if any), and treat it in terms of quantity."[1]

Why Does *The Abolition of Man* Matter?

Lewis originally prepared the text of *The Abolition of Man* as his script for the 1942 Riddell Memorial Lectures at the University of Durham. At the time he had achieved success as a fiction writer, and was becoming both one of the most influential authors of his time and a popular public intellectual. Lewis used the lectures to attack moral relativism and scientific reductionism* (the idea that a thorough scientific analysis of the processes and structures that constitute an organism is sufficient to fully understand it).

Indeed, he attacked these ideas in many of his works, including his novel *That Hideous Strength* (1945) and his essay "On Ethics," probably written in 1947. He challenged them by arguing that moral principles have an objective source that is not subject to human commentary or changing social rules.

Lewis's text is of special importance to both the student and the teacher. He stresses the power of education in shaping the minds of individuals, societies, and cultures, and hopes both to challenge teachers and to show them the effectiveness of their work. For him, education can change how a society functions. Good teaching leads to healthy societies; bad teaching threatens whole societies.

Lewis believes that an ideal education should teach students that values have a universal source and if there are universal truths, then it is harder to prize modern innovations over traditional values and world views. For Lewis, modern threats include propaganda, technology used as a way of dominating others, and manipulation of the natural world for the wrong purposes—and he includes the invention of the airplane, the radio, and birth control here. While contraceptive medicine may not strike contemporary readers as shocking, Lewis's arguments apply, too, to issues such as eugenics* (the application of genetic science to human populations in order to purposefully alter human traits) and biotechnology* (in which biological organisms and processes are scientifically exploited for human gain).

Lewis's defense of the natural world will likely resonate with students interested in modern ecological* and environmental questions. He links the treatment of the natural world to his broader moral claims and makes a robust philosophical plea for the sanctity of nature.

Lastly, the text is a classic example of the longstanding debate between theists* and atheists.* The American literary journal *National Review* ranked the book at number seven in its "100 Best Non-fiction Books of the 20th Century" list.

NOTES

1   C. S. Lewis, *The Abolition of Man* (New York: Harper San Francisco, 2001), 69.

SECTION 1
INFLUENCES

MODULE 1
THE AUTHOR AND THE
HISTORICAL CONTEXT

KEY POINTS

- *The Abolition of Man* is an engaging, spirited defense of the traditional morality found across religions and in philosophy and poetry.

- The text's values are founded on C. S. Lewis's love of poetry and nature, and on his Christian beliefs.

- Lewis reacted against the rise of logical positivism* (an approach to philosophy that challenges religious thought in its insistence that only verifiable statements have any value) and pragmatism* at his university, Oxford. This and his dismay at the ongoing World War II* prompted Lewis to write the essays that comprise *The Abolition of Man.*

Why Read This Text?

The three chapters that make up C. S. Lewis's *The Abolition of Man* were originally written as three Riddell Memorial Lectures delivered at the University of Durham in February 1942. These lectures, held annually since 1928, were always given by "a devout Christian, active throughout his life in public affairs." The intention was that they would deal with "the relation between religion and contemporary developments of thought."[1]

Lewis was already famous for his commercially successful Christian novel *The Screwtape Letters** (1942) and his lectures on BBC* radio about the nature and content of Christian religion. So he was considered an ideal speaker for an audience of theologians, clergymen, and academics who were sympathetic to his position as a

❝ All the books were beginning to turn against me. Indeed, I must have been blind as a bat not to have seen it long before, the ludicrous contradiction between my theory of life and my actual experiences as a reader. George MacDonald had done more to me than any other writer ... Chesterton* has more sense than all the other moderns put together; bating, of course, his Christianity. [Samuel] Johnson* was one of the few authors whom I felt I could trust utterly; curiously enough, he had the same kink. Spenser* and Milton* by a strange coincidence had it too. ❞

C. S. Lewis, *Surprised By Joy*, 1955

thinker working within the assumptions of the Church of England.*

Lewis used the lectures to attack moral relativism* (according to which it is impractical to say that one set of beliefs and actions is "more moral" than another) and scientific reductionism* (according to which the "mystery" of an organism is utterly irrelevant to, and can be explained away by, scientific analysis). Lewis wrote about these two philosophical standpoints in many of his works, including his novel *That Hideous Strength* (1945) and the posthumously published essay "On Ethics." He profoundly disagreed with these points of view, believing instead that moral principles have a source beyond human approval or the ever-changing fashions of society.

Although Lewis had outlined this moral philosophy in his BBC radio broadcasts, so that members of his audience would have already been familiar with his views, the lectures that became *The Abolition of Man* are the clearest illustration of his strongly held views on how a scientific world view was contributing to the decay of society. There were two factors he thought were particularly destructive: educating children to believe that value is a subjective matter they can decide for themselves; and the attempt to conquer and subdue nature through scientific and technological development.

These two ideas make Lewis's book relevant to equivalent debates in the twenty-first century.

Author's Life

Clive Staples Lewis (1898–1963), known as "Jack" by friends and family, was born in Northern Ireland in the city of Belfast. His childhood was marked by the death of his mother when he was just nine, and he spent the subsequent years bouncing from one school to another before returning home to study privately with his father's former schoolmaster. In 1916, Lewis won a scholarship to University College at Oxford, but World War I* disrupted his studies; between 1917 and 1918, he fought in the trenches of the Somme.* By 1923 he had completed his undergraduate studies in English, Greek, and Latin literature, as well as classical literature and philosophy.

He began his academic career at Oxford in 1924, as a fellow* of Magdalen College, and remained in Oxford as a lecturer and tutor in English until 1954. He spent his final years at the University of Cambridge, in the role of Professor of Medieval and Renaissance Literature—a post that had been specially created for him.

At Oxford, Lewis had the support and friendship of the literary group known as the Inklings.* The group's members included the scholar and author J. R. R. Tolkien* and the philosopher and poet Owen Barfield.* Like Lewis, these men immersed themselves in ancient mythological texts, and were enthusiastic about the genre of fantasy, believing it to be an excellent vehicle both for exploring old myths and for answering contemporary questions of society for both adult and child audiences.

Tolkien helped to motivate Lewis's slow and reluctant conversion to Anglican Christianity* over the period of 1929 to 1931.

Author's Background

In February 1942, Lewis was invited to deliver the Riddell Memorial Lectures at the University of Durham. He gave a series of three evening lectures that were later published as *The Abolition of Man*.

The title strongly suggests the work's chief theme: Lewis's fears for the downfall of the human race. He believed that the deterioration of morality at the time—with people treating fellow humans as objects to manipulate, control, or use merely as the means to an end—could have such an outcome. For him, one of the worst symptoms of this trend was the decreasing standard of moral education, which explains the lengthy subtitle: *Reflections on Education with Special Reference to the Teaching of English in the Upper Forms of Schools.*

In the text, Lewis takes issue with the practice of teaching schoolchildren that value is a matter of personal attitudes, or subjective ideas. In contrast, he argues that there is an objective moral standard applicable to all individuals. Referencing a Chinese religious philosophy according to which we are obliged to live according to laws that acknowledge the moral structure inherent in the universe, Lewis calls this standard "the Tao,"* or "natural law,"* saying that it "is the sole source of all value judgements. If it is rejected, all value is rejected."[2] *The Abolition of Man* is a striking statement of his conviction that human society faces destruction unless there is a return to educating children about true values.

A number of social factors frustrated Lewis and motivated his writing. He begins by discussing how English was being taught in senior schools at the time. He goes on to question the recently developed contraceptive pill, dismissing it as a form of technology that enables one generation to control the next.

Lewis wrote the book while serving in the Home Guard* (the domestic defense forces during World War II, usually exempt from active service on account of their age); his work and travel were unaffected since Oxford was not subjected to air raids. He was, however, concerned about the control, manipulation, and propaganda that occurred during wartime and he raises these factors, too, in *The Abolition of Man*.

NOTES

1   E. J. Furlong, "Languages, Standpoints and Attitudes: Riddell Memorial Lectures, at the University of Durham by H. A. Hodges," *Hermathena* 84 (1954): 113.

2   C. S. Lewis, *The Abolition of Man* (New York: Harper San Francisco, 2001), 43.

MODULE 2
ACADEMIC CONTEXT

KEY POINTS

- *The Abolition of Man* argues for a universal moral law that can be used in both education and philosophy.

- Lewis's morality is traditional and challenges the modern moral philosophies popular at Oxford University at the time.

- While Lewis had a great interest in philosophy and religion, he was never officially a part of any philosophy or religion faculty, being a professor of English.

The Work in its Context

The themes of C. S. Lewis's *The Abolition of Man* include philosophy, morality, and education. Lewis was particularly concerned with the philosophical ideas that were popular in Britain in the 1940s. His belief in traditional morality put him at odds with certain movements then dominating philosophical studies at Oxford University: logical positivism* and pragmatism.*

Pragmatism, a school of thought that developed in the 1870s, stresses the practicality or usefulness of ideas or knowledge rather than essential truths. Logical positivism, which developed in the 1920s and 1930s, focuses on ridding philosophy of anything that could not be proven by factual evidence or through logical deduction—an idea that basically counted out religious philosophy altogether, since it was founded on unverifiable scripture. Originally popular in Germany and Austria, logical positivism's supporters moved to the United States and Britain, particularly after the rise of the right-wing German Nazi* party.

Philosophers working within both these schools of thought

> ❝ Their [Lewis's opponents'] scepticism about values is on the surface: it is for use on other people's values; about the values current in their own set they are not nearly sceptical enough. And this phenomenon is very usual. A great many of those who 'debunk' traditional or (as they would say) 'sentimental' values have in the background values of their own which they believe to be immune from the debunking process. ❞
>
> C. S. Lewis, *The Abolition of Man*

regarded Lewis's idea of a universal morality and meaning beyond human understanding as out of date and illogical.

Overview of the Field

The Abolition of Man is a work that crosses a number of disciplines, including philosophy, religion, literature, and education. Lewis looks back centuries, even millennia, to major thinkers and ideas from many past cultures, taking in Ancient Greek philosophy, Hinduism,* Christianity,* mythology, and English poetry. He thought Ancient Greek philosophers and Christian theologians shared many of the same values. Similarly, he found Christian values harmonized with themes from poetry and mythology. These were views shared by fellow members of his literary circle known as the Inklings,* and by the slightly earlier Scottish Christian poet and writer of fantasy and fairy tales, George MacDonald.*

Lewis's work belonged within this specific literary community; all of the other writers in it used theology* (the systematic study of the nature of God), myth, fantasy, and poetry in their writings, too. Like Lewis, they were all concerned that their readers, and society at large, should not give more importance to science, rationality, and pragmatism than they gave to beauty, myth, storytelling, and mystery.

The Abolition of Man is also important on a theological level, and it defends the Christian world view (even if Lewis believes that this world view is not unique to Christianity). In this sense, *The Abolition of Man*, together with the rest of Lewis's work, compares to that of G. K. Chesterton,* a noted Catholic writer of fiction and non-fiction.

Academic Influences

As a teenager, C. S. Lewis was enthralled by Icelandic mythology,* Norse sagas,* and ancient lyrical poetry.* The tutor who prepared him for university, William T. Kirkpatrick, encouraged his interest in Classical Greek* literature. The references to old Irish history in the poetry of the Irish poet W. B. Yeats* similarly fascinated him. George MacDonald's books encouraged Lewis's own love of mythology as well as his later tendency to stress the mysterious and unfathomable over all forms of naturalism* (according to which the universe is governed by moral laws).

The Abolition of Man reflects Lewis's love of ancient tradition and myth and his belief that human understanding is not a matter of scientific analysis but one of universal morality—that is, the idea that there is a natural law* defined by constant, universal moral principles, which must be followed if we are to make good moral judgments.

For Lewis, this is a belief that is present in a number of ancient religions, schools of thought and traditions, including the ancient Chinese practice and philosophy of Taoism,* and the philosophies of Aristotle* and Plato.* In his essay "On Ethics,"[1] which covered similar ground to *The Abolition of Man*, Lewis stresses that his work does not demand a total return to ancient principles; referring to the Ancient Greek philosophy of Stoicism,* according to which human action should be strongly moderated, he writes that he was not "trying to reintroduce in its full Stoical or medieval rigour the doctrine of Natural Law."[2] He does, however, deny that humans can make their own new system of morality. He wrote that "wherever and whenever ethical discussion begins we find already before us an ethical code whose validity has to be assumed before we can even criticize it."[3]

NOTES

1   C. S. Lewis, "On Ethics," in *Christian Reflections*, ed. Walter Hooper (Grand Rapids: Eerdmans, 1967).

2   Lewis, "On Ethics," 55.

3   Lewis, "On Ethics," 55.

MODULE 3
THE PROBLEM

KEY POINTS

- The central question of *The Abolition of Man* is: "On what do we base morality?"

- Lewis believes that morality is rooted in a universal, unchanging source. His opponents argued instead that it could be based only on scientific truth, factual evidence, or pragmatism* (the position that an idea should be valued on the extent to which it has a practical application).

- Lewis systematically rejects all of his opponents' views, including the possibility of humans creating their own moral values based on scientific knowledge, pragmatism, or usefulness.

Core Question

At the heart of *The Abolition of Man* are two questions. The first is: "Does morality have a source that is beyond human invention or subjective thinking?" Lewis's answer to this fundamental and ancient question is decisive: we must accept a belief in a universal moral value beyond our own making. In making his argument, Lewis refers to a number of traditional sources, including Plato,* Aristotle,* and the Chinese concept of the Tao* (literally, "the way," indicating, very roughly, a certain understanding of the cosmos that requires a lived moral response).

The second question Lewis asks is: "What will happen to human society if we teach our children that value is subjective?" His answer to this is, of course, linked to the first question. He begins his argument on this point by mentioning two contemporary textbooks designed

❝ For the wise men of old the cardinal problem had been how to conform the soul to reality, and the solution had been knowledge, self-discipline and virtue. For magic and applied science alike the problem is how to subdue reality to the wishes of men: the solution is a technique; and both, in the practice of this technique, are ready to do things hitherto regarded as disgusting and impious—such as digging up and mutilating the dead. ❞

C. S. Lewis, *The Abolition of Man*

to help schoolchildren in English lessons. Lewis disapproves of both of these books because they undermine traditional morality, teaching that statements of value are really just about someone's emotional state.

Over the course of his three chapters, Lewis argues that this flawed approach to morality in the modern education system is no trivial matter. In fact, it is a form of social conditioning that is sinister in its scope. He writes that "the practical result of education in the spirit of [these contemporary textbooks] must be the destruction of the society which accepts it."[1] In this sense, in *The Abolition of Man* Lewis is giving his own novel answer to Plato's famous question "Can virtue be taught?" Lewis's view is that modern society is producing "men without chests" (the title of his first chapter)—people who don't have the ability to be virtuous, because their value system is built on a faulty, subjective set of principles.

The Participants

The Abolition of Man is a text of moral philosophy—though Lewis was not part of the philosophy department of Oxford University.

Followers of pragmatism,* logical positivism* (deeply invested in rational analysis above all else), and the behaviorist* philosopher and lecturer Gilbert Ryle* (who emphasized the importance of observing physical behavior since the mind was by definition invisible) rejected the core concept in Lewis's work that moral principles have an objective and divine source.

They defined meaningful language and meaningful philosophical claims as being capable of being proven by sensory experience or scientific observation. They thought that Lewis's notion—that the source of moral principles is objective and lies beyond all human approval or analysis—was simply meaningless. Moreover, his references to such traditional philosophical figures as Plato and the Christian thinker Augustine* served only to demonstrate his distance from these newer modern movements.

In spite of the antagonism between Lewis and his colleagues in philosophy, Lewis himself was always enthusiastic about the subject and, as a postgraduate student, he wrote in one of his diaries about his hope of attaining a fellowship* in philosophy. This never happened; he ended up specializing in the study of literature.

It was in these diaries, we also find, that he began to develop the ideas he would eventually present in *The Abolition of Man*, including the core concept of moral objectivity (according to which, roughly, when we talk about morality, we are talking about something that exists outside the human mind).

The Contemporary Debate

C. S. Lewis addresses broad and weighty issues in *The Abolition of Man*, among them scientific reductionism* (the notion that an organism is nothing more than can be explained by a scientific analysis that takes no account of its "mystery"), naturalism* (according to which the universe is governed by moral laws), emotivism* (the idea that moral statements have more to do with your emotional state than they do with "truth"), and moral relativism* (the idea that no moral framework is better than any other). As one critic observes, he argues energetically that behind the modern world's constantly changing attitudes and fashions, there remains "a primordial nucleus of values whose destruction would mean the destruction of the human species itself."[2]

Lewis argues that his contemporaries are losing their sense of true objective value in denying those moral principles that transcend time and place. Citing the Chinese philosopher Confucius,* the Roman theorist Cicero,* the Ancient Greeks, and the Bible, Lewis positions himself as the inheritor of an ancient set of philosophical insights and denies that he is a moral innovator.

In fact, innovation is precisely what he is against—and he challenges several new schools of thought.

In the first chapter of *The Abolition of Man,* Lewis attacks emotivism, a prominent school of thought in the 1940s advocated by the philosopher A. J. Ayer* in his book *Language, Truth and Logic* (1936). Although Lewis does not mention any of his contemporary opponents by name, one of his reviewers pits him against the American philosopher John Dewey.* Dewey supported pragmatism—a philosophical movement that emerged in the United States in the 1870s and rejected the notion that thought and language faithfully represent reality.

Lewis's other opponents included the pragmatist philosopher Wilfred Sellars,* who completed his MA at Oxford University in 1940 and who observed that Lewis—then working at Oxford—was in an environment that favored Dewey's disciples.

The behaviorist philosopher Gilbert Ryle, whose rational positions were certainly incompatible with much of Lewis's thought, was also a philosophy lecturer at Oxford when Lewis wrote the book.

NOTES

1   C. S. Lewis, *The Abolition of Man* (New York: Harper San Francisco, 2001), 27.

2   Rodica Albu, "C. S. Lewis: *The Abolition of Man,*" *JRSI* 15 (Winter 2006): 110.

MODULE 4
THE AUTHOR'S CONTRIBUTION

KEY POINTS

- Lewis believed that modern philosophy and education were based on numerous falsehoods and failings.

- The only way to combat these problems was by understanding that morality was objective and based on old—and even ancient—teachings.

- While Lewis's argument in *The Abolition of Man* is original in its prose and style, and in the way he weaves together traditional teachings, the underlying concepts rely on earlier thinkers.

Author's Aims

C. S. Lewis originally delivered *The Abolition of Man* as a set of evening talks—the Riddell Memorial Lectures—at the University of Durham in 1942. He was invited to speak under the general guidelines that he must "treat of the relation between religion and contemporary developments of thought."[1] According to one commentator, Lewis set about this task on a grand scale, setting out "to attack and confute what he saw as the errors of his age"[2]— namely, the positions of moral subjectivism* (according to which the individual can choose what is true and what is false, independent of any universal moral law), naturalism,* and scientific reductionism.*

For Lewis, these three views were simply false—symptoms of modern society's loss of respect for teaching a true and objective morality.

Lewis himself had long been convinced of the value of this teaching and by 1942 he had already written various academic papers

> **❝** Man's conquest of Nature, if the dreams of some scientific planners are realized, means the rule of a few hundreds of men over billions upon billions of men. There neither is nor can be any simple increase of power on Man's side. Each new power won by man is a power over man as well. Each advance leaves him weaker as well as stronger. **❞**
>
> C. S. Lewis, *The Abolition of Man*

and given numerous lectures. These included his postgraduate dissertation on moral authority, his radio broadcasts entitled "Right and Wrong," and his paper for the Oxford Socratic Club, "If We Have Christ's Ethics Does the Rest of the Christian Faith Matter?" The Socratic Club was a debating society focused on philosophical ideas, and, as its president, Lewis, then a lecturer in the English faculty at Oxford University, attended all its meetings. During these sessions he became increasingly anxious about the impact of such current philosophical movements as logical positivism* and emotivism.*

Approach

By the time he wrote *The Abolition of Man*, Lewis was already a celebrated speaker, and the clarity of his thinking had resulted in an invitation to give a series of talks on BBC* radio and to deliver the Riddell Memorial Lectures. The ideas in the book, too, are expressed innovatively; Lewis combines philosophical reasoning with witty, even sometimes sarcastic, prose to make his arguments accessible and convincing—but they were not in themselves original. Indeed, they symbolized the concerns of the age.

Earlier in 1931, the British author Aldous Huxley* had expressed his unease about the implications of the scientific world view in his novel *Brave New World*. Huxley depicts a fictional human society in which impressive technologies seem to improve the quality of human life and happiness; this so-called happiness, however, comes at a terrible price: it results in the end of human freedom, diversity, and culture. Like Huxley, Lewis does not offer a tangible set of solutions to the problems he diagnoses.

Lewis's antipathy to scientific reductionism has even earlier influences, such as the poets of the English Romantic movement* (a movement particularly concerned with the capacity of the natural world to move us), in particular the poet Samuel Taylor Coleridge,* whose world view is echoed in *The Abolition of Man*. Lewis, in fact, is not trying to contribute new points to the ongoing debate about the problems with scientific reductionism and naturalism. Instead, he sees himself as part of an already established tradition of thinkers that includes Coleridge and, later, G. K. Chesterton,* a Christian author and theologian.*

Contribution in Context
C. S. Lewis relied on ideas from a number of other thinkers and traditions in *The Abolition of Man*, constantly referencing the work of others in his text. Aiming to link his disparate sources in a united common philosophy, Lewis's own originality lies in the way he harmonizes their ideas to this effect. He connects philosophies from across centuries and cultures—for example, the philosophy of the Indian religion of Hinduism,* that of the Ancient Greeks, and English poetry in the following lines: "Righteousness, correctness, order, the *Rta*, is constantly identified with *satya* or truth, correspondence to reality. As Plato said that the Good was 'beyond existence' and Wordsworth that through virtue the stars were strong, so the Indian masters say that the gods themselves are born of the *Rta* and obey it."[3]

Although Lewis's approach and philosophy do not in themselves form a "school of thought," *The Abolition of Man* does reflect concerns that were shared by Lewis's friends and peers in the Inklings,* the group of Oxford writers that met regularly and that included J.R.R. Tolkien* and the writer Owen Barfield.* The group was inspired by figures such as G. K. Chesterton and the Scottish fantasy author George MacDonald;* all of its members were interested in writing modern fairy tales, myths, and works of fantasy. In *The Abolition of Man*, Lewis portrays a natural world that is no longer treated as if it had a beauty or life of its own worthy of respect—instead, it is there to be used, even destroyed, solely for human purposes. This echoes, in Lewis's own unique way, the concern common to all the members of the Inklings about the toxic spread of the scientific world view within contemporary culture.

NOTES

1   E. J. Furlong, "Languages, Standpoints and Attitudes: Riddell Memorial Lectures, at the University of Durham by H. A. Hodges," *Hermathena* 84 (1954): 113.

2   J. R. Lucas, "The Restoration of Man," *Theology* (November/December 1995): 445–56.

3   C. S. Lewis, *The Abolition of Man* (New York: Harper San Francisco, 2001), 17.

SECTION 2
IDEAS

MODULE 5
MAIN IDEAS

KEY POINTS

- C. S. Lewis is concerned about how schools teach morality to children and the effect on human society.

- Lewis believes that we must hold on to objective values or we will lose our way both philosophically and morally.

- Lewis's three essays form a witty and sharp attack on bad education and subjectivism* (the idea that we are all capable of deciding what is "true" ourselves, without acknowledging any universal moral law).

Key Themes

The book's full title is *The Abolition of Man, or Reflections on Education with Special Reference to the Teaching of English in the Upper Forms of Schools*—illustrating C. S. Lewis's two main themes, education and human nature. Lewis also includes a discussion of the status or quality of contemporary society, and this, he believes, is under threat, even "abolition" (total annulment). Lewis's focus on morality is another thread running through all of his arguments. He analyzes how modern educators fail to teach a "doctrine of objective value, the belief that certain attitudes are really true, and others really false."[1] It is this failure, he argues, that is making people, as adults, unable to behave in a virtuous and fruitful way.

Lewis's argument can be summarized as a rejection of moral relativism.* He describes the tendency of the age to teach children that value and morality are subjective—meaning that someone's responses to an object or event are merely down to personal opinion. Lewis contrasts this approach with traditional, and in some cases ancient, ways

> ❝ This conception in all its forms, Platonic,*
> Aristotelian,* Stoic,* Christian,* and Oriental alike,
> I shall henceforth refer to for brevity simply as 'the
> *Tao*'.* Some of the accounts of it which I have
> quoted will seem, perhaps, to many of you merely
> quaint or even magical. But what is common to
> them all is something we cannot neglect. It is the
> doctrine of objective value, the belief that certain
> attitudes are really true, and others really false, to
> the kind of thing the universe is and the kind of
> things we are. ❞
>
> C. S. Lewis, *The Abolition of Man*

of conceiving what is meant by the moral life, all of them involving a belief in objective value, something beyond the merely personal and subjective. These traditions include Christianity, represented by the founding theologian* Augustine,* and the English literary tradition of Romanticism,* represented by the poet Samuel Taylor Coleridge.*

Lewis's ideas, in fact, require an understanding of the ideas of Augustine and Coleridge, as well as those of the Greek philosophers Plato* and Aristotle,* all of whom Lewis regards as crucial thinkers in the history of moral philosophy.

Perhaps most of all, though, Lewis is interested in the Chinese concept of the Tao, which points to a reality which exists beyond all human understanding, and represents "the Way in which things everlastingly emerge."[2]

Exploring the Ideas

The Abolition of Man has three chapters. In the first, Lewis focuses on education, identifying a major problem with English teaching in the secondary schools of his day. He cites two textbooks that, he says, tell their readers that meaning is subjective—that "all sentences containing a predicate [that is, an assertion] of value are statements about the emotional state of the speaker." Lewis argues that these textbooks are effectively communicating to young minds that we should focus on the emotions we experience as individuals rather than on the true, objective nature of other people and the world around us.

In chapter two, Lewis proposes that this type of teaching is inadequate if his generation wants to pass on to the next a knowledge of, and respect for, true moral goodness. He turns to the theme of morality and demonstrates how his own belief in objective moral value differs from that of modern "innovators" such as the authors of the English textbooks. According to Lewis, these innovators want to abandon traditional moral teaching—such as that found in the work of Coleridge, or in Taoist texts—that requires both reason and contemplation. Instead, he writes, these modern authors suggest that human desires and behaviors are shaped by "instincts" which, for him, cannot be a cohesive or consistent source of moral behavior. Indeed, for Lewis, "Our instincts are at war."[3]

Lewis's third chapter turns to "the abolition of man" that forms the title of the book. He begins by examining the breakdown of belief in objective value and morality. This, he believes, results in an attitude that dismisses the world as mere nature, something that exists solely for each individual to use for his or her own needs. The natural world, comprising plants and animals, is reduced to something of no significance, there merely for humans to control or conquer. The final outcome must be that humans will treat each other in the same destructive way.

Language and Expression

As a whole, Lewis's *Abolition of Man* is logical, coherent, and well structured—no doubt helped by the fact that it was originally written as a three-part public lecture series. But although the text is short and easy to read, not assuming any expertise on the part of the reader, there are a number of literary and cultural references that may be unfamiliar to some readers—in particular, the many references to classical works and authors. There are also references to British society and to the politics of the day. Lewis is primarily interested in identifying trends in education and morality, and in showing how these trends are harmful. He doesn't analyze specific theories or pick out academic opponents, choosing instead to discuss his themes using terms such as "the Innovators" and "the Conditioners." The first of these terms refers to people who depart from traditional moral values. The second features in Lewis's depiction of society's future leaders, who, convinced of their mission to control nature, go on to apply the same harmful conditioning to the human race.

Modern readers may find Lewis's style, manner, and language outdated in his constant references to "man" or "men," for example, rather than to the more neutral "humanity." As his biographer A. N. Wilson* suggests, it is possible that today's readers of Lewis's book will find "an affectedly old-fashioned, crusty man with a pipe and a lot of male cronies who is going to complain about any modern developments in thought, knowledge or understanding."[4] While this may be an exaggeration, it is true that the culture of Lewis's Oxford University does belong to a very different era.

NOTES

1   C. S. Lewis, *The Abolition of Man* (New York: Harper San Francisco, 2001), 43.

2   Lewis, *The Abolition of Man*, 18.

3   Lewis, *The Abolition of Man*, 36.

4   A. N. Wilson, *C. S. Lewis: A Biography* (London: Collins, 1990), 197.

MODULE 6
SECONDARY IDEAS

KEY POINTS

- Lewis contends that scientific reductionism* has two terrible by-products. The first is the loss of enchantment and wonder; the second is that it encourages striving for power, both over nature and over other people.

- These two by-products threaten the hypothetical schoolchild that Lewis discusses in his critique of moral subjectivism.*

- With hindsight, Lewis's ideas about humanity's quest for power through the subjugation of nature or people are considered farsighted in view of today's technological developments and ecological problems.

Other Ideas

The Abolition of Man is an attack on the linked perspectives of scientific reductionism and naturalism,* which, as C. S. Lewis understands them, can be described as "the movement by which things came to be understood simply as parts of nature, objects that have no inherent purpose or *telos*, which therefore become resources available for human use" (by "telos" he is referring to an end that justifies something's existence).[1]

In delivering his argument against such reductionism, C. S. Lewis introduces two secondary themes.

The first is his dissatisfaction with the loss of what other scholars, such as the Canadian philosopher Charles Taylor,* have since called an "enchanted" perspective on the world—meaning a belief that the world around us has a life independent of human

> ❝ What we call Man's power [over nature] is, in reality, a power possessed by some men which they may, or may not, allow other men to profit by. ❞
>
> C. S. Lewis, *The Abolition of Man, or Reflections on Education with Special Reference to the Teaching of English in the Upper Forms of Schools*

knowledge, wishes, and intentions. In his final chapter, Lewis blames both industry and the scientific world view for bringing about this disenchantment, arguing that "we do not look at trees either as Dryads* or as beautiful objects while we cut them into beams." And, Lewis continues, "the stars lost their divinity as astronomy developed."[2]

Lewis's description of this opposition between science and magic brings us to his second subordinate idea, which concerns power. For Lewis, humanity's quest for power over nature is tragic, because it pushes human society towards its own destruction. We are, says Lewis, mortal, finite creatures who are not in control of our own futures, and we cannot know the eventual outcome of even simple scientific innovations. He writes that "each new power won by man is a power over man as well. Each advance leaves him weaker as well as stronger. In every victory, besides being the general who triumphs, he is also the prisoner who follows the triumphal car." [3] In making this point, Lewis echoes Samuel Taylor Coleridge,* a Romantic* poet and philosopher deeply concerned about the impact of both nature on humans and humans on nature.

Exploring the Ideas

Although Lewis believes that we should understand nature as living and active, this does not mean he is sympathetic to the idea of magic. In fact, he sees magic as the twin of science, "born of the same impulse." Science and magic, he thinks, both result in humans manipulating nature, and scientists, just like witches and magicians, "are ready to do things hitherto regarded as disgusting and impious—such as digging up and mutilating the dead."[4]

Two other related ideas emerge in Lewis's analysis of moral relativism.* The first is that the scientific world view leads to a desensitization in attitudes towards both the natural world and humanity itself. He argues that there is a natural tendency in scientific practice towards reductionism and objectification* (that is, reducing something to the status of a mere object), since "when we understand a thing analytically and then dominate and use it for our own convenience, we reduce it to the level of 'Nature' in the sense that we suspend our judgments of value about it, ignore its final cause (if any), and treat it in terms of quantity."[5] For Lewis, the aim of science is to manipulate reality so that it conforms to human desires. Science is not only anthropocentric (interpreting everything in terms of human experience and values), it also assumes—wrongly, Lewis believes—that humans are in charge of their own futures.

Lewis's second key idea concerns technology as the means by which science is able to conquer nature and subdue it. He investigates the precarious relationship between modern technology and humanity, concluding that his contemporaries will make later generations weaker than themselves, rather than stronger, "for though we may have put wonderful machines in their hands we have pre-ordained how they are to use them."[6] Lewis sees the contraceptive pill as the prime example of a dangerous innovation, his generation actively dictating the composition of those to come and wielding influence, paradoxically, over those who are not yet alive.

Overlooked

The Abolition of Man received little attention on its publication in 1943. Originally, the entire work was overlooked, although a number of C. S. Lewis's friends, among them the essayist Owen Barfield,* praised the book for its strong argument and its excellent writing style. In addition, Lewis received many positive reviews from the clergy and the theological academic community, who agreed with his "vindication of Natural Law,* not as demonstrable, but as absolute, standing in its own right", and who also thought that the book displayed a "finely philosophical mind."[7] Nevertheless, all of this agreement and praise did not amount to a serious or critical dialogue.

In fact, Lewis's philosophical opponents did not judge his newest text to be worthy of their scrutiny at all. The logical positivists,* pragmatists,* and behaviorists* who populated the faculty of philosophy at the University of Oxford (Lewis was based in the faculty of English) were so unimpressed that Lewis clung to such traditional, well-established, and, by that time, outmoded notions that they ignored him. It was not merely Lewis's traditional approach that discouraged criticism—his unforgiving and brisk style contributed to this too. Although he mounted a powerful attack on what he saw as the threats of moral relativism, scientific reductionism, and naturalism, Lewis failed to properly engage with, or represent, the particular positions taken up by his philosophical opponents. Because he merely simplified their arguments—and thereby made them easier to dismiss—his opponents didn't see his attack as a real threat, and simply ignored it.

Nowadays, though, most commentators see the book as remarkably farsighted. Logical positivism has long been superseded by approaches with a more nuanced relation to rational analysis, and Lewis's critique of moral subjectivism has more support today. Contemporary critics, among them the American Christian philosopher Peter Kreeft,* see the text as ripe for reconsideration, praising Lewis for his insightful view that both reductionism and the idea of technological progress inevitably lead to the opinion that the natural world has no inherent worth and is simply there for human use and manipulation.

NOTES

1   Gilbert Meilaender, "On Moral Knowledge," in *The Cambridge Companion to C. S. Lewis*, eds. Robert MacSwain and Michael Ward (Cambridge: Cambridge University Press, 2010), 128.

2   C. S. Lewis, *The Abolition of Man* (New York: Harper San Francisco, 2001), 70.

3   Lewis, *The Abolition of Man*, 58.

4   Lewis, *The Abolition of Man*, 77.

5   Lewis, *The Abolition of Man*, 69.

6   Lewis, *The Abolition of Man*, 57.

7   Philip Leon, "The Abolition of Man," *The Hibbert Journal* 42 (1944): 280–2.

MODULE 7
ACHIEVEMENT

KEY POINTS

- C. S. Lewis launched a concise, well-conceived attack on moral relativism,* identifying its effects on the individual, on society, and on nature.

- Lewis's fine prose and remarkable knowledge of literature, philosophy, and theology together produce a persuasive, cultivated text.

- Lewis's traditional morality alienated him from his contemporaries, who ignored his philosophical and moral ideas.

Assessing the Argument

The lectures that eventually became C. S. Lewis's *The Abolition of Man* were written to defend traditional morality and moral objectivism.* One of the ways Lewis did this was by challenging three perceived scientific advances of the time—the radio, the airplane, and the contraceptive pill—arguing that there was a more sinister potential to each seemingly positive technology.

The radio, he argued, can be used as a means of spreading propaganda; the airplane most benefits the wealthy and powerful who can afford it; and the pill allows for the potentially coercive suppression of unborn children. These three examples are the most succinct among those given by Lewis in a much larger attack on technology and scientific reductionism;* together, they highlight the importance, for Lewis, of humans having a moral framework for understanding the world around them.

Over his three talks, Lewis defended his view that morality

> ❝[C. S. Lewis] set out to attack and confute what he saw as the errors of his age. ❞
>
> J. R. Lucas, "The Restoration of Man"

and values are objective. In the first, he tackled what he saw as "materialist and anti-religious indoctrination creeping into education."[1] In the second, he explained what traditional objective morality is, and how the same basic beliefs are shared by all of the great religions and philosophical schools. Lewis's third and final lecture was an attack on scientific reductionism; in it, he outlined the problems it would cause for the future of human society.

Lewis was a famous and accessible public speaker and he put his views across vividly and convincingly. There is a confused element, though, in his second chapter where he "[lumps] together … the traditional moralities of East and West, the Christian, the Pagan,* and the Jew."[2] In order to further his argument against subjectivism* and relativism, Lewis suggests that in all of the religious traditions he includes—as well as in the philosophies of Plato,* Aristotle,* and the Stoics*—value was understood to be objective. But while Lewis emphasizes the similarities in these traditions, he fails to point out their significant differences in practice.

Achievement in Context

Notwithstanding the neglect that Lewis's book received from his contemporaries at Oxford University and from academics further afield, the Anglican* (Church of England) community endorsed his work (even if he was literally preaching to the converted). Lewis's argument and his concept of objective moral values were steeped in the Anglican tradition. Contemporary philosophers, champions of logical positivism* and pragmatism,* ignored him, thinking that he was not making any contribution to modern philosophy.

Those in philosophical circles tended to regard Lewis, since he was in the English Department at Oxford University, as irrelevant. While Lewis had studied philosophy as an undergraduate, he would spend his entire life in literature faculties; in terms of philosophy, he was, essentially, an outsider. It was not until years later that *The Abolition of Man* would receive any serious attention, and that was at least in part due to the popularity of Lewis's fiction, especially *The Chronicles of Narnia*.* Since this increase in attention, *The Abolition of Man* has been translated into a number of European languages.

Limitations

C. S. Lewis's forceful attack on moral relativism and naturalism* was in many ways a product of its time—the text was written in war-torn Britain—and some of its themes no longer seem relevant today. One of the main philosophical movements he sought to undermine, logical positivism, has long ceased to be active or significant. In addition, the fascist and communist regimes that Lewis cites as contemporary threats to freedom in Europe have long since collapsed. However, since the economic crisis of 2007–8, extremist parties across Europe have increased in popularity and Lewis's anxieties about propaganda and public manipulation are suddenly relevant again in this shifting and increasingly polarized political landscape.

Lewis's concern that people in a society governed according to the principles of scientific reductionism will "come to be motivated simply by their own pleasure"[3] continues to be relevant in the modern context of capitalism* and the global consumer society. He does not, however, tackle economic themes or the role of the market in shaping human desires, matters which would seem most relevant today; his focus is on how the human sense of "value" has deteriorated due to subjectivist philosophy and the scientific world view.

Despite these limitations, the consensus on *The Abolition of Man* today is that it displays remarkable foresight about the negative side of the impulse to produce increasingly impressive and efficient machines and gadgets, the products of new technologies intended to improve the quality of human life.

NOTES

1   Roger Lancelyn Green and Walter Hooper, *C. S. Lewis: A Biography* (London: Collins, 1974), 174.

2   C. S. Lewis, *The Abolition of Man* (New York: Harper San Francisco, 2001), 44–5.

3   Lewis, *The Abolition of Man*, 65.

MODULE 8
PLACE IN THE AUTHOR'S WORK

KEY POINTS

- C. S. Lewis's career was prolific. His constant aim was to defend traditional morality, ideas of beauty, Christianity, and the importance of wonder and enchantment.

- *The Abolition of Man*, a mid-career work, presents the clearest statement of his views on morality and modern society.

- Although *The Abolition of Man* is less popular than Lewis's other works, such as *The Screwtape Letters** and *The Chronicles of Narnia,** it is still widely read today.

Positioning

One of the recurring themes in C. S. Lewis's *The Abolition of Man* concerns the threat that humans pose to themselves and the natural world. Society will destroy itself, he predicts, if we turn entirely to naturalist* thought; by reducing our understanding of the universe to something produced by natural physical forces alone, we will eventually lose any conception of objective morality. Such destruction, he explains, will amount to a gradual "process whereby man surrenders object after object, and finally himself, to Nature in return for power."[1]

In the foreword to his 1946 novel *That Hideous Strength*, Lewis explains that the story's message makes the same warning and that it should be read alongside *The Abolition of Man*. Both books reveal Lewis's particular interest in Chinese Taoist* philosophy, with its conception of a reality that exists beyond all human understanding. One of Lewis's commentators, Gilbert Meilaender, cites the Tao

> **❝ [*That Hideous Strength*] has behind it a serious 'point' which I have tried to make in my *Abolition of Man.* ❞**
> C. S. Lewis, *That Hideous Strength, A Modern Fairy-Tale for Grown-Ups*

(defined as "the Way in which things everlastingly emerge")[2] as a major concept in *That Hideous Strength*. In it, the protagonist experiences the principles of the Tao as "the starting point for all moral reasoning, deliberation and argument; that is, they are to morality what axioms are to mathematics. They are not conclusions, but premises."[3]

There are also interesting parallels between *The Abolition of Man* and the themes in *The Chronicles of Narnia** (1950–6). In both, Lewis warns against teaching children to believe that value is subjective, while he depicts magic, just like modern science, as a force for "[subduing] reality to the wishes of men."[4]

The theme of disenchantment can be found not just in *The Abolition of Man* but also in the three novels of Lewis's earlier *Space Trilogy** (1938–45); these books have been characterized as a struggle against the naturalistic perspective.

Integration

C. S. Lewis published his first book in 1919 and continued to write prolifically until his death in 1963. His work includes novels, poetry, essays, academic texts, and his autobiography, *Surprised by Joy* (1955). *The Abolition of Man*, an attack on moral relativism* originally devised as a set of three evening lectures, was published in 1943; this period during World War II was an especially productive time for Lewis. It is possible he felt a heightened sense of responsibility to the peoples of Europe, attuned to their trauma and distress.

Between 1940 and 1947 he published *The Problem of Pain*, a work on the Christian response to suffering; the book *Mere Christianity*;

an essay titled "Miracles"; and the commercially successful Christian novel *The Screwtape Letters*.* The ideas in these works are all connected, reflecting Lewis's tendency to write on the same core themes, such as love, suffering, morality, and human nature. All of the books also broadly address the problem of living as a committed Christian in modern Western society. As much as Lewis loathed the naturalist point of view, he saw it gaining ground over his own theistic* respect for an objective morality—a perspective grounded in the belief that the universe has been created by a loving God.

Unlike these other books, Lewis did not write *The Abolition of Man* from a specifically Christian perspective. While his academic contemporaries and the public mostly ignored it when it was first published, Lewis himself regarded it as an important work. Certainly, it is a lucid and impassioned essay that distilled his thinking to that point about the state of morality in the Western contemporary world, and that was also an examination of an idea he would go on to explore in one of his later novels.

Significance

Having enjoyed success with *The Screwtape Letters*, Lewis was also renowned at that time for his lectures on BBC* radio on Christian matters. He was certainly an ideal speaker for the three Riddell Memorial Lectures he delivered at the University of Durham in February 1942 to an audience made up theologians, clergymen, and academics, sympathetic to his position as a traditional Anglican* thinker.

Lewis used the lectures (and the versions of those lectures printed as *The Abolition of Man*) to attack moral relativism and scientific reductionism,* philosophical viewpoints he denounced in many of his works, and to defend the idea that moral principles have an objective source beyond human argument. Without this objective source, morality and society would, he believed, be vulnerable to mere whim and changing fashions. Lewis had clearly outlined this moral philosophy in his BBC radio broadcasts, so interested members of his audience would already have been familiar with his views by the time *The Abolition of Man* was published.

The Abolition of Man is arguably the clearest statement of Lewis's views on these matters. He saw two underlying problems in particular: the tendency to educate children to believe that value and morality are subjective; and the attempt to conquer and subdue nature through scientific analysis and technological development.

The book is regularly compared to Aldous Huxley's* 1932 novel *Brave New World*, with its warnings of how a combination of scientific rationality and social conditioning can shape society in a profoundly harmful manner. The theologian Alister McGrath* has even written that *The Abolition of Man* marks Lewis out as a "prophet."[5]

NOTES

1 C. S. Lewis, *The Abolition of Man* (New York: Harper San Francisco, 2001), 76.

2 Lewis, *The Abolition of Man*, 18.

3 Gilbert Meilaender, "On Moral Knowledge," in *The Cambridge Companion to C. S. Lewis*, eds. Robert MacSwain and Michael Ward (Cambridge: Cambridge University Press, 2010), 120.

4 Lewis, *The Abolition of Man*, 77.

5 Alister McGrath, *C. S. Lewis: A Life, Eccentric Genius, Reluctant Prophet* (London: Hodder & Stoughton, 2013).

SECTION 3
IMPACT

MODULE 9
THE FIRST RESPONSES

KEY POINTS

- Lewis's critics saw his traditional perspective as old-fashioned and irrelevant.

- Fans of C. S. Lewis, including academics, authors, and Christians, praised his defense of moral objectivism.*

- As Lewis's fame grew because of his other work, both fiction and non-fiction, *The Abolition of Man* was saved from obscurity.

Criticism

Critical responses to C. S. Lewis's *The Abolition of Man* came broadly from two groups.

The first group was made up of friends, admirers of his existing essays and popular fiction, and academics who approved of his attack on naturalism* and moral relativism* and his argument that moral principles have an objective and timeless source. They all agreed that the text was excellently written and persuasive and showed, as one reviewer said, "a finely philosophical mind which makes … rings round unphilosophical and, indeed, mindless minds." [1] If, for some of this group, the book was an astute and worrying assessment of contemporary attitudes, they were not generally vocal about this—perhaps because, as J. R. Lucas,* a commentator on Lewis's work, suggested, he "was reminding his audience of what they already knew, and drawing out the implications of propositions they already accepted."[2]

The second group was made up of philosophers, social scientists, and other academics who rejected Lewis's argument that moral

> ❝ In 1947, we still believe our 'realism' is directed
> towards some desirable goal. Unless humanity
> makes an abrupt about-face, it seems likely that our
> grandchildren will have no goals. ❞
>
> Chad Walsh, "The Abolition of Man," *New York Herald Tribune Book Review*

value is objective (that is, that morality exists independently of our
subjective, personal conceptions of what is moral and what is not).
They were supporters of the currents in contemporary philosophy
known as logical positivism* and pragmatism*—then new and
increasingly popular positions which opposed Lewis's traditional
morality, and which were incompatible with Lewis's argument that
objective moral values lie outside human understanding or control.

Logical positivists, such as the influential philosopher A. J.
Ayer,* argued that statements had meaning only if they could be
proved by sensory observation, or, as with mathematical theorems,
demonstrated by logic. So when Lewis argued in *The Abolition of
Man* for the meaningfulness of terms such as "goodness," "beauty,"
"evil," and "ugliness," the logical positivists and the pragmatists
denounced such terms as unscientific and, as a result, unable to tell
us anything about the external world.

Responses

C. S. Lewis was offered little constructive or critical feedback for
The Abolition of Man.

It is very safe to assume that he was supported by those, such as
his close friend and fellow Inkling* Owen Barfield,* who agreed
with his philosophical positions; Barfield wrote to him saying that
the book was "a real triumph" which brought together "precision
of thought, liveliness of expression and depth of meaning."[3] But
other than Barfield's endorsement, there is little evidence of any

kind of response to the work. Lewis received thousands of letters in response to his BBC lectures, and it is possible that the Riddell Lectures elicited responses in the form of private correspondence. However, it is certain that there was no serious written response from the academic world or from Lewis's community at Oxford.

One potential explanation for the lack of scholarly response to the text is the ambiguity of Lewis's role as a philosopher. Although he deals with philosophical concepts in many of his works, as an academic he was a specialist in literature and philology. As such, despite his presidency of the Socratic Club—a society that existed to debate "the intellectual difficulties connected with religion"—religious Oxford philosophers may not have considered him their peer within the field of philosophy. [4] Despite this lack of scholarly response, Lewis was confident of the importance of his arguments in *The Abolition of Man* and would echo its claims in a number of subsequent works.

Conflict and Consensus

C. S. Lewis never retracted any of the ideas he proposed in *The Abolition of Man*, and in his subsequent fiction and non-fiction he continued to highlight the moral, social, and aesthetic cost of the scientific world view. This unswerving commitment did not, however, influence his detractors. Those philosophers who dismissed Lewis's arguments as outmoded because they opposed the new philosophical schools of pragmatism, logical positivism, and behaviorism continued to reject Lewis's approach as outmoded and flawed and, wary of his reputation as a popular Christian thinker, they gave Lewis's book negligible critical attention in public debate or in their own published material.

The somewhat terminal decline in the popularity of the new philosophical schools was unrelated to Lewis's criticisms of them. In a sense, therefore, the philosophical landscape changed before any consensus between them could be reached.

Given the unfashionable nature today of the pragmatic, logical positivist, and behaviorist schools of thought, modern readers know little about them and are often unaware of them as a context for Lewis's work. *The Abolition of Man* is usually read as a general critique of technology and a defense of traditional values, although modern readers may find it difficult to understand Lewis's view of radios, airplanes, and oral contraceptives as threats to society.

NOTES

1 Philip Leon, "The Abolition of Man," *The Hibbert Journal* 42 (1944): 280–2.

2 J. R. Lucas, "The Restoration of Man," *Theology* (November/December 1995): 445–56.

3 Walter Hooper, *C. S. Lewis: A Companion and Guide to His Life and Works* (London: Fount, 1996), 341.

4 Oxford University Socratic Club, "The Socratic Digest," 1 (1942–43): 6.

MODULE 10
THE EVOLVING DEBATE

KEY POINTS

- Decades after publication, many readers agree with Lewis's idea that the modern world has seen an increasingly dangerous relationship develop between science, technology, the natural world, and humanity.

- Although *The Abolition of Man* did not generate any new schools of thought, it did bolster the arguments of those, religious or otherwise, who support traditional moral world views.

- The book's popularity has grown since its publication, and it is now seen as a forceful and engaging outline of Lewis's philosophy as well as a farsighted vision of society that still applies in the twenty-first century.

Uses and Problems

In his critically acclaimed biography of C. S. Lewis, published in 2013, the Oxford professor of science and religion Alister McGrath* notes that *The Abolition of Man* was, and remains, one of Lewis's "less popular works."[1] But while he admits it is a difficult book, McGrath also believes that "its arguments remain highly significant,"[2] and he gives a brief summary of its influence on later discussions about the nature of moral value and the threat of scientific reductionism*— the topics which mostly preoccupied Lewis.

The Abolition of Man cannot really be called a game changer. It failed to make much of an impact when it was published, nor did it take a significant role in shaping or fueling the moral and philosophical debates of the time. It is true that some of the

❝ *[The Abolition of Man]* is an important book: nothing less than an analysis of where and how the modern world has gone wrong. **❞**
A. N. Wilson, *C. S. Lewis: A Biography*

philosophical schools that Lewis opposed in 1940—notably pragmatism,* logical positivism,* and behaviorism*—have since collapsed, but Lewis and his work were not significant factors in their demise. And another school he particularly challenged, that of naturalism,* is still in the mainstream of both the philosophy of science and philosophy more generally today. Influential public intellectuals of our own time, such as Richard Dawkins* and Stephen Hawking,* would strongly oppose Lewis's appeal to an eternal source of objective moral principles—a source that transcends the natural world—although neither have engaged with him.

Within Christian circles and the academic disciplines of Christian ethics and philosophy of religion, however, there are a few notable modern commentators, such as McGrath, who are sympathetic to Lewis's position. They believe that he was remarkably astute in his presentation of scientific naturalism as a harmful culture that would lead to the unsustainable view that humans are rightfully the consumers, manipulators, and masters of nature.

Schools of Thought

C. S. Lewis's *The Abolition of Man* was originally commissioned as a series of three evening lectures, in which Lewis was asked to "treat of the relation between religion and contemporary developments of thought."[3] With such a broad brief, it is not surprising that the text is of interest to those from a range of academic disciplines, including religious studies, theology,* philosophy, and education.

The book's breadth, though, has meant that its influence on these disciplines has been minimal and it has generated no real academic dialogue in any discipline, nor has it generated any new schools of thought. Nowadays, its influence could be best described in terms of providing a compelling, thought-provoking source of inspiration for those studying moral philosophy and Christian* theology, especially those working at an undergraduate level. Lewis does not introduce a new or innovative moral standpoint. Instead, he examines the traditional belief that human morality has an objective and abiding source—a teaching that he identifies as being common to Platonic* and Aristotelian* philosophy and the Christian religion.

Likewise, *The Abolition of Man* has failed to have a major influence on experts in education, politics, social theory, or science. Commentators from these disciplines and within philosophy have all appeared indifferent to the book and have failed to respond to it critically or constructively.

In Current Scholarship

The Abolition of Man does not introduce a new philosophy so much as it defends a traditional one, and so, academically, it is not seen as playing a part in the evolution of or debate about European philosophy.

Lewis may not have created a new school of thought, but since the height of his career in the 1940s and 1950s, he has been admired by millions beyond the academic world.

Viewed within Lewis's work as a whole, *The Abolition of Man*'s significance is as a manifesto giving his views on morality, on contemporary education, and on flawed moral teaching that educates young people to believe that value is subjective. In it, Lewis sets out both his ideas and the prediction that this flawed morality will lead ultimately to the destruction of a functioning and well-organized society.

Those practicing philosophers who admire Lewis—or who are at least willing to discuss his ideas—hold, like Lewis himself, traditional

Western views on morality and the concept of objective value. Most of his supporters write from the perspective of Christian belief.

Academics who have published work on Lewis since 2000 include Alister McGrath, the former Archbishop of Canterbury Rowan Williams,* Lewis's close friend Owen Barfield,* and Michael Ward,* who is a senior research fellow at Blackfriars, a center for the study of theology in Oxford. Professor Peter Kreeft* of Boston College stated, in the mid-1990s, that the book was one of six that everyone should read in the interests of preserving Western civilization.

NOTES

1 Alister McGrath, *C. S. Lewis: A Life, Eccentric Genius, Reluctant Prophet* (London: Hodder & Stoughton, 2013), 369.

2 McGrath, *C. S. Lewis*, 231.

3 E. J. Furlong, "Languages, Standpoints and Attitudes: Riddell Memorial Lectures, at the University of Durham by H. A. Hodges," *Hermathena* 84 (1954): 113.

MODULE 11
IMPACT AND INFLUENCE TODAY

KEY POINTS

- *The Abolition of Man* is a compelling argument against moral relativism* and a concise and important introduction to the thought of C. S. Lewis.

- *The Abolition of Man* challenges supporters of moral relativism by showing the threat such a world view poses to humanity and the natural world.

- Fans of C. S. Lewis believe his defense of traditional values answers new moral dilemmas posed by scientific innovations in today's world.

Position

C. S. Lewis's *The Abolition of Man* can be summed up as an attack on scientific reductionism,* naturalism,* and moral relativism. Lewis predicts the downfall of all human societies that live by such rules—societies which, in other words, condition their children to believe that they can choose their own values, and where the natural world is merely a resource to be used for human benefit.

The particular philosophical schools of thought that Lewis confronted in 1942—logical positivism* and pragmatism*— are now obsolete and forgotten. Lewis's ideas in *The Abolition of Man* are, though, still relevant today, particularly in terms of the debate about the effects of science and technology on society. Indeed, the present day may well fulfill many of Lewis's worst fears; he would probably regard the vast and globally significant scientific industries of biotechnology* and genetic engineering as ways in which human beings have come to

❝ If any book is able to save us from future excesses of folly and evil, it is this book. ❞

Walter Hooper, quoted in Rodica Albu's "C. S. Lewis: The Abolition of Man"

establish themselves as manipulators, controllers, and exploiters of the natural world.

Many modern readers find that Lewis's concerns about scientific reductionism remain relevant today. Generally, though, *The Abolition of Man* still does not arouse much interest from the scientific and philosophical communities, and apart from one recent article in the *Journal of Evolution and Technology*, there has been no significant academic response to Lewis's arguments. That article, "The Invention of Man: A Response to C. S. Lewis's *The Abolition of Man*," considered how Lewis's arguments were relevant in light of such potential modern technologies as: "neuroscience,* drugs, computerized implants, brain-machine interfaces, mind uploading, nanoscale* devices, and other advanced technologies."[1] The author argued that while Lewis's warnings about science were important, ultimately we should be trusted to use technology for progress and the advancement of the species.

Beyond the academic world, there is a greater appreciation for Lewis's warning about the eventual demise of a society that treats the world, including the people in it, as a set of resources to be exploited and plundered.

Interaction

The widespread popularity of C. S. Lewis's other work (his children's fantasy novels, and especially *The Chronicles of Narnia**) means that *The Abolition of Man* is still read today, especially by those interested in morality, theology, literature, and the meeting point of philosophy and science. It is particularly popular with

Christian readers, whether Anglican* (as Lewis was) or of other denominations. It appeals more, though, to a popular readership than to a scientific or academic one, remaining largely ignored by the academic world.

The book's importance has emerged with the passage of time. Out of all of Lewis's body of work, it gives the clearest and most academic presentation of two of themes that were especially important to him—the importance of universal morality, and the dangers of thinking about the world in a reductive* or naturalistic way. Although commentary still remains generally limited to popular thought pieces, lectures, and occasional articles, in the mid-1990s the philosopher Peter Kreeft* published a collection of essays about the book titled *C. S. Lewis for the Third Millennium: Six Essays on* "The Abolition of Man", the first essay in which was titled "How to Save Western Civilization."

The Continuing Debate

Modern-day scientists and supporters of the scientific world view such as Richard Dawkins* have never engaged directly with Lewis, and *The Abolition of Man* is not part of the established debate about the role of science in society. It would be difficult for those coming from a scientific background to argue against Lewis's position, given that there is no common ground between them, and because Lewis is so fiercely opposed to their ideas. This is complicated by the fact that they would not be opposing C. S. Lewis alone; Lewis did not speak as an individual but as one among an extremely broad range of philosophers and traditions, including Plato,* Aristotle,* and Augustine,* all of whom agreed that value, including moral value, is objective.

Lewis's book and its arguments remain relevant to undergraduates studying theology and philosophy and to Christian readers generally; it continues to be read by fans of his fiction, too.

A number of academics and prominent figures place *The Abolition of Man* among the most influential books they have ever read; among these are Peter Kreeft and the American Christian writer Charles Colson,* who described it as his favorite essay.

NOTES

1   Gregory E. Jordan, "The Invention of Man: A Response to C. S. Lewis's *The Abolition of Man*," *Journal of Evolution and Technology* 19, no. 1 (September 2008): 35.

MODULE 12
WHERE NEXT?

KEY POINTS

- *The Abolition of Man* continues to captivate students, especially at the university level, and those interested in the importance of education.

- It remains a compelling debate about values and the threats posed by science and technology to humanity and the natural world.

- It makes a powerful argument for an objective morality and provides a manifesto for those who want to challenge naturalism* and scientific reductionism* today.

Potential

Given C.S. Lewis's legacy as a defender of the Christian faith, children's author, and successful novelist, it is unlikely that *The Abolition of Man*, in itself a lively and excellently written essay, will lose its readership soon. Far from seeing it as out of date, Lewis's current readers usually find his arguments against scientific reductionism* and moral relativism* highly relevant. This is evident in the sociologist Brian Gareau's 2013 work on environmental issues,[1] while the American Christian author Charles Colson* believed that *The Abolition of Man* had prophetic powers.

"C. S. Lewis," Colson said, "a professor of medieval literature, was a true prophet in the sense that he saw then what others could not. In his great book *The Abolition of Man*, Lewis critiqued what he saw as the triumph of science over humanity, warning that this would bring about 'the abolition of man,' turning him into a project and product."[2]

> **❝** *[The Abolition of Man]* **is almost my favourite among my books, but in general has been almost totally ignored by the public. ❞**
> C. S. Lewis to Mary Willis Shelburne, *Collected Letters*

Part of that "prophetic" quality lies in Lewis's warnings about the practice of exploiting nature and the development of technologies and scientific processes that—like the contraceptive pill—give certain people the power to control the nature and composition of future generations. These ideas now seem particularly relevant given developments in research that today allow us to manipulate genes and to alter biological processes, and concerns about global warming and the future of our planet's ecosystems. Lewis's book is regularly compared to the British author Aldous Huxley's* famous novel *Brave New World* in which a society brings about its own demise when sophisticated technology apparently created for the benefit of human happiness becomes a means for a minority to assume power over the many.

While Lewis sets out the problem, he does not offer any solutions. His work predicts the demise of human society due to moral relativism and scientific reductionism but he makes no suggestions about how the problems might be solved. The book, then, is better at provoking debate than it is at solving the problems it envisions, which might deter some readers. Modern readers could also be alienated by Lewis's outdated style, manner, and language.

Future Directions

For today's admirers of Lewis's work, *The Abolition of Man* is unsettlingly prophetic, not least in its prediction of a future society in which "man by eugenics,* by pre-natal conditioning, and by an education and propaganda based on a perfect applied psychology, has obtained full control over himself."[3] It is a vision of a conditioned and controlled humanity that can still be used to challenge modern investments in genetic engineering and biotechnology. As Lewis's biographer A. N. Wilson* commented in 1990, "this is an important book: nothing less than an analysis of where and how the modern world has gone wrong."[4]

Lewis discussed the social and moral implications of the contraceptive pill—a major scientific breakthrough of his time—but there are now many more complicated scenarios of scientifically assisted human reproduction (in-vitro fertilization, surrogacy, three-donor pregnancies). Lewis's concerns about such possibilities make *The Abolition of Man* particularly relevant to modern readers. As ecological disasters and environmental changes in the world repeatedly highlight the fragility of humanity's relationship with nature, Lewis's disgust at the exploitation of the natural world inspires his readers today to question how natural resources are used or misused.

In the year 2000, the American literary magazine *National Review* listed *The Abolition of Man* as number seven in its list of the top 100 best non-fiction books of the twentieth century. In 2010, the Intercollegiate Studies Institute judged the book to be the second best book of the twentieth century, and enduringly relevant.

Summary

When C. S. Lewis published *The Abolition of Man* in 1943, his friends and admirers and many contemporary scholars of religious philosophy judged it a remarkable book, both well written and prophetic. It was an in-depth critique of the current standard of education in British schools, an indictment of scientific reductionism and naturalism, and a prediction of the destruction of human society that these perspectives would bring about. Writing during World War II,* and in this time of crisis, his warnings about exploiting, manipulating, and conquering the natural world did not appear to constitute an original or innovative academic work. Instead, as was Lewis's aim, the book was seen as a powerful and accessible manifesto for the preservation of traditional moral values. In 1947, one reviewer explained how Lewis had convinced him that "unless humanity makes an abrupt about-face, it seems likely that our grandchildren will have no goals. They will love or hate, caress or kill, as irrational nature dictates."[5]

With a well-established legacy extending well beyond the book itself, C. S. Lewis is still admired by millions. Indeed, as a popular literary figure, children's author, and defender of Christian faith, his reputation goes far beyond the boundaries of the academic community and professional scholars. On the fiftieth anniversary of his death in 2013, a special commemorative service was held for him in Westminster Abbey. A sermon was given by the former Archbishop of Canterbury, Rowan Williams,* and a memorial plaque was installed, so that Lewis's name appears alongside those of other literary giants, such as Geoffrey Chaucer* and Edmund Spenser.*

NOTES

1   Brian J. Gareau, *From Precaution to Profit: Contemporary Challenges to Environmental Protection in the Montreal Protocol* (New Haven: Yale University Press, 2013).

2   Charles Colson and Nigel M. de S. Cameron, eds., *Human Dignity in the Biotech Century: A Christian Vision for Public Policy* (Downers Grove: InterVarsity Press, 2004), 17.

3   C. S. Lewis, *The Abolition of Man* (New York: Harper San Francisco, 2001).

4   A. N. Wilson, *C. S. Lewis: A Biography* (London: Collins, 1990), 197.

5   Chad Walsh, "The Abolition of Man," *New York Herald Tribune Book Review*, April 13, 1947, 5.

GLOSSARIES

GLOSSARY OF TERMS

Anglicanism: the Christian denomination comprising the Church of England and those other Churches that belong to the international Anglican Communion.

Aristotelian: the philosophy of Aristotle (384–322 B.C.E.), a classical Greek philosopher and student of Plato. Aristotle's writings have profoundly influenced Christian theology, as well as Western political thought and the dramatic arts. Famous works of his include *The Poetics* and *Nicomachean Ethics*.

Atheist: one who does not believe in the existence of a "supreme being" or god.

BBC: the British Broadcasting Corporation, a license-funded institution responsible for providing unbiased broadcasting via television, radio, and the Internet for the British public.

Behaviorism: thinkers in the behaviorist school maintain, broadly, that in the process of analyzing human behavior, philosophers should give their foremost attention to observable behaviors, such as muscular movements, over non-observable mental phenomena, such as thoughts and beliefs.

Biotechnology: the process of harnessing biological systems or living organisms in order to develop useful techniques or products.

Capitalism: an economic system based on private ownership, private enterprise, and the maximization of profit.

Christianity: one of the major world religions along with Islam, Hinduism, Buddhism, and Judaism. It is based on the life and teachings of Jesus Christ in the first century C.E., recorded in the New Testament of the Bible.

Church of England: also known as the Anglican Church, this is the branch of Christianity founded in England by King Henry VIII in the sixteenth century.

Classical Greek: the period from the sixth to the fourth century B.C.E. when Greek culture flourished; it is known for great works of art, philosophy, poetry, and drama.

Dryad: the female spirits of Greek mythology who lived in trees.

Ecological: relating to the environment, and particularly the relations of living things to each other or within systems.

Emotivism: a theory according to which ethical statements merely reflect emotional states, rather than carrying an objective truth. A famous advocate of emotivism was the British thinker A. J. Ayer.

Eugenics: the scientific practice of altering a population through the mechanism of controlled breeding, to the end of bringing about an increased level of a desired characteristic, such as blonde hair color or hazel eye color.

Fellow: a position in a British university that grants one both teaching and governing responsibilities.

Hinduism: a polytheistic religion found primarily in India and South Asia, which first developed in around 1500 B.C.E.

Home Guard: British reserve forces of World War II, made up of men who were usually exempt from active service on account of their age and tasked with defending their homeland in the event of an invasion by enemy forces.

Icelandic mythology: the ancient and medieval stories of the people of Iceland.

Inklings: an informal literary group associated with the University of Oxford, England, from the early 1930s until 1949. They were enthusiastic about fiction, particularly fantasy, and counted among their number C. S. Lewis, J. R. R. Tolkien, and Owen Barfield.

Logical positivism: a theory about human knowledge that emerged out of Austria and Germany in the 1920s. It is characterized by the view that coherent human language and communication is grounded in actual, verifiable statements.

Lyrical poetry: a form of poetry that primarily expresses emotions and feelings, often in the first person.

Moral objectivism: the idea that a system of ethics or values has inherent truth and can be followed universally, independent of time, geography, culture, and so on.

Moral relativism: in its broadest sense, this is the idea that standards differ depending on the time, place, or culture that one is occupying. According to this theory, no one action can be objectively right or wrong.

Nanoscale: on the atomic or molecular scale.

Naturalism: the view that the universe is governed by natural laws that dictate its structure and behavior. According to this view, no supernatural or mysterious explanatory account is either required or coherent.

Natural law: the idea of unchanging moral principles used to guide individual action and to determine the obligations of people and institutions.

Nazi: the National Socialist Party; a racist, authoritarian, and extremely right-wing German political party led by Adolf Hitler until the end of World War II.

Neuroscience: science concerned with the brain and the nervous system.

Norse sagas: the long and often heroic stories of ancient Scandinavian peoples.

Objectification: the process by which one uses things or people for one's own gain without recognizing any inherent value.

Pagan: a series of historical religious traditions, most of which involve the worship of many gods.

Platonic: the philosophy of Plato (427–347 B.C.E.), a classical Greek philosopher, founder of the Academy in Athens, and arguably the most important and influential author in the history of Western thought. His works include *The Republic* and *Phaedrus*.

Pragmatism: broadly, this refers to a philosophical movement that emerged out of the United States in the 1870s. Its core teaching was that the meaning of ideas is contained in the practical significance of adopting them.

Protestantism: one of the major forms of Christianity, with its own doctrines and practices, of which the Anglican Church forms a part.

Romanticism: an artistic movement current between 1789 and 1850. Among its key figures in English literature were Samuel Taylor Coleridge, William Wordsworth, William Blake, and John Keats. These writers opposed the reduction of nature to a set of objects for humanity to control, emphasizing instead the beauty of the natural world and its ability to affect or change us.

Reductive: presenting a subject or problem in a simplified form.

Scientific reductionism: broadly, this refers to the philosophical perspective whereby an organism or system is understood as the sum total of its constituent parts, so that nothing "mysterious" remains beyond what the scientific account can make of it.

Somme: the Battle of the Somme, or the Somme Offensive, was one of the longest and bloodiest battles of World War I.

Space Trilogy: a series of science fiction novels by C. S. Lewis, also known as the *Cosmic Trilogy*, published between 1938 and 1945.

Stoicism: a movement in Greek philosophy founded in the third century B.C.E. The Stoics stressed the importance of not being susceptible to strong emotions.

Subjectivism: the concept that it is the subject, or an individual, who is the one who decides what the truth is, rather than truth existing independently from the individual.

Tao: literally "the way" or "the path," indicating, very roughly, a certain understanding of the cosmos that requires a lived moral response.

The Chronicles of Narnia: a seven-part series of fantasy novels for children by C. S. Lewis. They were written between 1949 and 1954 (published between 1950 and 1956) and have since sold 100 million copies in 47 languages.

Theism: the belief in a higher power or god responsible for designing the universe and possibly still governing it.

Theology: the systematic study of the nature of God.

The Screwtape Letters: is a satirical work of fiction by C. S. Lewis (1942) written as a series of letters between two demons.

World War I (1914–18): the global armed conflict between the Allied powers (Britain, France, Russia, and the United States) on the one side and the Central Powers (Germany, the Ottoman Empire, and Austria-Hungary) on the other.

World War II (1939–45): the global armed conflict between the Allied powers (Britain, France, Russia, and the United States) and the Axis powers of Germany, Italy, Japan, and their satellite states.

PEOPLE MENTIONED IN THE TEXT

Aristotle (384–322 B.C.E.) was a classical Greek philosopher and student of the philosopher Plato, whose writings have profoundly influenced Christian theology, Western political thought, and the dramatic arts. His famous works include *The Poetics* and *Nicomachean Ethics*.

Augustine of Hippo (354–430) was a philosopher, theologian, and African bishop, considered one of the foremost influences upon the tradition of Western Christianity. His important works include *Confessions*, *City of God*, and *De Trinitate*.

A. J. Ayer (1910–89) was a British philosopher, known for his adherence to the logical positivist movement and his book *Language, Truth and Logic* (1936).

Owen Barfield (1898–1997) was a British writer, philosopher, and poet.

Geoffrey Chaucer (1343–1400) was an extremely influential English poet, author, and philosopher. His most famous works include *The Canterbury Tales* and *Troilus and Criseyde*.

Gilbert Keith Chesterton (1874–1936) was a British poet, essayist, and lay Christian theologian, famous for his books on Christian apologetics (texts written to justify Christian faith), including *The Everlasting Man* (1925) and *Orthodoxy* (1908).

Marcus Tullius Cicero (106–43 B.C.E.) was a Roman philosopher, politician, lawyer, orator, and political theorist. He came from a wealthy Roman family and is considered one of the great Roman writers and orators. His writings were especially influential for eighteenth-century European philosophers.

Samuel Taylor Coleridge (1772–1834) was an English philosopher, essayist, poet, and founding member of the English Romantic movement. He saw nature as an organic whole, full of energy, and he believed Christianity and the natural sciences opened up truths about nature. Best known for his long poem *Rime of the Ancient Mariner*, his most famous work of philosophy is the *Biographia Literaria* (1817).

Charles Colson (1931–2012) was a former American government advisor imprisoned for his role in the political scandal known as "Watergate," which brought down the administration of President Richard Nixon in 1974. Colson later converted to Christianity. He became a popular author and a major voice in American Evangelicalism.

Confucius (fifth century B.C.E.) was a Chinese teacher, philosopher, and politician. Confucianism, or the philosophy of Confucius, emphasizes personal and governmental morality, justice, and sincerity.

Richard Dawkins (b. 1941) is an evolutionary biologist, popular science writer, famous atheist, and professor emeritus of Oxford University. Famous publications of his include *The Selfish Gene* (1976) and *The God Delusion* (2006).

John Dewey (1859–1952) was an American philosopher, best known for his association with the philosophical position of pragmatism.

Stephen Hawking (b. 1942) is a cosmologist, theoretical physicist, popular science writer, and researcher at the University of Cambridge. His most famous and widely read book is *A Brief History of Time* (1988), which has sold more than 8 million copies.

Aldous Huxley (1894–1963) was an English author and essayist whose most famous novel is *Brave New World* (1932).

Samuel Johnson (1709–84) was an English author, critic, poet, and Anglican moralist, best known perhaps for his *A Dictionary of the English Language* of 1755, considered a spectacular feat of scholarship.

Peter Kreeft (b. 1937) is a professor of philosophy at Boston College and The King's College in New York City. He is the author of numerous books on Christian philosophy, theology, and apologetics (texts written to justify Christian faith).

J. R. Lucas (b. 1929) is a British philosopher. Best known perhaps for his paper "Minds, Machines and Gödel," he is an emeritus member of the Faculty of Philosophy at Oxford University and a Fellow of the British Academy (Britain's national academy for the humanities and the social sciences).

George MacDonald (1824–1905) was a Scottish poet, novelist, essayist, and Christian clergyman. He was the author of *The Princess and the Goblin* (1872).

Alister McGrath (b. 1953) is from Northern Ireland. He is a theologian, priest, intellectual historian, scientist, and Christian apologist (writing texts to justify Christian faith), as well as producing works on science and religion. At present he holds the Andreas Idreos Professorship in Science and Religion in the Faculty of Theology and Religion at the University of Oxford.

John Milton (1608–74) was an English poet. He is best known for his epic poems *Paradise Lost* (1667) *and Paradise Regained* (1671).

Plato (427–347 B.C.E.) was a classical Greek philosopher, founder of the Academy in Athens, and arguably the most important and influential author in the history of Western thought. His works include *The Republic* and *Phaedrus*.

Gilbert Ryle (1900–76) was a British philosopher famous for his critique of the French philosopher René Descartes (1596–1650) and his view that it is not tenable to speak about humans in terms of a mind–body dualism. His work includes *The Concept of Mind* (1949).

Wilfred Sellars (1912–89) was an American philosopher interested in the philosophy of mind. He was the author of *Philosophy and the Scientific Image of Man* (1962).

Edmund Spenser (1552–99) was an English poet, best known for his epic poem *The Faerie Queen*.

Charles Taylor (b. 1931) is a philosopher and Roman Catholic from Canada. Professor emeritus at McGill University, he is notable for his works on political philosophy and the philosophy of social science.

J. R. R. Tolkien (1892–1973) was a British fantasy author, poet, and professor of English literature. A Roman Catholic, he is famous worldwide for his *Lord of the Rings* trilogy (1954–5).

Michael Ward (b. 1968) is a British scholar. Senior research fellow at Blackfriars, Oxford, he is best known for his book *Planet Narnia*, a discussion of the structure of Lewis's *The Chronicles of Narnia*.

Rowan Williams (b. 1950) is an Anglican bishop, theologian, and poet. He was the Archbishop of Canterbury from 2002 to December 2012.

Andrew Norman Wilson (b. 1950) is an English writer and newspaper columnist, known for his views on religion. As well as critical biographies, he has written novels and popular historical works.

William Butler Yeats (1865–1939) was an Irish poet and winner of the Nobel Prize for Literature in 1923. Among his famous work is *The Tower* (1928).

WORKS CITED

WORKS CITED

Albu, Rodica. "C. S. Lewis: *The Abolition of Man*." *Journal for the Study of Religions and Ideologies* 15 (Winter 2006).

Atkins, Peter. "The Limitless Power of Science." In *Nature's Imagination*, edited by John Cornwell. Oxford: Oxford University Press, 1995.

Colson, Charles, and Nigel M. de S. Cameron, eds. *Human Dignity in the Biotech Century: A Christian Vision for Public Policy*. Downers Grove: InterVarsity Press, 2004.

Furlong, E. J. "Languages, Standpoints and Attitudes: Riddell Memorial Lectures, at the University of Durham by H. A. Hodges." *Hermathena* 84 (1954).

Gareau, Brian J. *From Precaution to Profit: Contemporary Challenges to Environmental Protection in the Montreal Protocol*. New Haven: Yale University Press, 2013.

Hooper, Walter. *C. S. Lewis: A Companion and Guide to His Life and Works*. London: Fount, 1996.

Jordan, Gregory E. "The Invention of Man: A Response to C. S. Lewis's *The Abolition of Man*." *Journal of Evolution and Technology* 19, no. 1 (September 2008): 35–41.

Kreeft, Peter. "How to Save Western Civilization." In *C. S. Lewis for the Third Millennium: Six Essays on "The Abolition of Man"*, by Peter Kreeft. San Francisco: Ignatius Press, 1994.

Lancelyn Green, Roger, and Walter Hooper. *C. S. Lewis: A Biography*. London: Collins, 1974.

Leon, Philip. "The Abolition of Man." *The Hibbert Journal* 42 (1944): 280–2.

Lewis, C. S. *Miracles: A Preliminary Study*. New York: HarperCollins, 2009.

————. "On Ethics." In *Christian Reflections*, edited by Walter Hooper. Grand Rapids: Eerdmans, 1967.

————. *Surprised by Joy: The Shape of My Early Life*. New York: Harcourt, Brace, Jovanovich, 1966.

————. *That Hideous Strength, A Modern Fairy-Tale for Grown-Ups*. New York: Macmillan Publishing Company, 1946.

————. *The Abolition of Man*. New York: Harper San Francisco, 2001.

Lucas, J. R. "The Restoration of Man." *Theology* (November/December 1995).

McGrath, Alister. *C. S. Lewis: A Life, Eccentric Genius, Reluctant Prophet*. London: Hodder & Stoughton, 2013.

Meilaender, Gilbert. "On Moral Knowledge." In *The Cambridge Companion to C. S. Lewis*, edited by Robert MacSwain and Michael Ward. Cambridge: Cambridge University Press, 2010,

Walsh, Chad. "The Abolition of Man." *New York Herald Tribune Book Review*, April 13, 1947.

Wilson, A. N. *C. S. Lewis: A Biography*. London: Collins, 1990.

THE MACAT LIBRARY
BY DISCIPLINE

AFRICANA STUDIES

Chinua Achebe's *An Image of Africa: Racism in Conrad's Heart of Darkness*
W. E. B. Du Bois's *The Souls of Black Folk*
Zora Neale Huston's *Characteristics of Negro Expression*
Martin Luther King Jr's *Why We Can't Wait*
Toni Morrison's *Playing in the Dark: Whiteness in the American Literary Imagination*

ANTHROPOLOGY

Arjun Appadurai's *Modernity at Large: Cultural Dimensions of Globalisation*
Philippe Ariès's *Centuries of Childhood*
Franz Boas's *Race, Language and Culture*
Kim Chan & Renée Mauborgne's *Blue Ocean Strategy*
Jared Diamond's *Guns, Germs & Steel: the Fate of Human Societies*
Jared Diamond's *Collapse: How Societies Choose to Fail or Survive*
E. E. Evans-Pritchard's *Witchcraft, Oracles and Magic Among the Azande*
James Ferguson's *The Anti-Politics Machine*
Clifford Geertz's *The Interpretation of Cultures*
David Graeber's *Debt: the First 5000 Years*
Karen Ho's *Liquidated: An Ethnography of Wall Street*
Geert Hofstede's *Culture's Consequences: Comparing Values, Behaviors, Institutes and Organizations across Nations*
Claude Lévi-Strauss's *Structural Anthropology*
Jay Macleod's *Ain't No Makin' It: Aspirations and Attainment in a Low-Income Neighborhood*
Saba Mahmood's *The Politics of Piety: The Islamic Revival and the Feminist Subject*
Marcel Mauss's *The Gift*

BUSINESS

Jean Lave & Etienne Wenger's *Situated Learning*
Theodore Levitt's *Marketing Myopia*
Burton G. Malkiel's *A Random Walk Down Wall Street*
Douglas McGregor's *The Human Side of Enterprise*
Michael Porter's *Competitive Strategy: Creating and Sustaining Superior Performance*
John Kotter's *Leading Change*
C. K. Prahalad & Gary Hamel's *The Core Competence of the Corporation*

CRIMINOLOGY

Michelle Alexander's *The New Jim Crow: Mass Incarceration in the Age of Colorblindness*
Michael R. Gottfredson & Travis Hirschi's *A General Theory of Crime*
Richard Herrnstein & Charles A. Murray's *The Bell Curve: Intelligence and Class Structure in American Life*
Elizabeth Loftus's *Eyewitness Testimony*
Jay Macleod's *Ain't No Makin' It: Aspirations and Attainment in a Low-Income Neighborhood*
Philip Zimbardo's *The Lucifer Effect*

ECONOMICS

Janet Abu-Lughod's *Before European Hegemony*
Ha-Joon Chang's *Kicking Away the Ladder*
David Brion Davis's *The Problem of Slavery in the Age of Revolution*
Milton Friedman's *The Role of Monetary Policy*
Milton Friedman's *Capitalism and Freedom*
David Graeber's *Debt: the First 5000 Years*
Friedrich Hayek's *The Road to Serfdom*
Karen Ho's *Liquidated: An Ethnography of Wall Street*

The Macat Library By Discipline

John Maynard Keynes's *The General Theory of Employment, Interest and Money*
Charles P. Kindleberger's *Manias, Panics and Crashes*
Robert Lucas's *Why Doesn't Capital Flow from Rich to Poor Countries?*
Burton G. Malkiel's *A Random Walk Down Wall Street*
Thomas Robert Malthus's *An Essay on the Principle of Population*
Karl Marx's *Capital*
Thomas Piketty's *Capital in the Twenty-First Century*
Amartya Sen's *Development as Freedom*
Adam Smith's *The Wealth of Nations*
Nassim Nicholas Taleb's *The Black Swan: The Impact of the Highly Improbable*
Amos Tversky's & Daniel Kahneman's *Judgment under Uncertainty: Heuristics and Biases*
Mahbub Ul Haq's *Reflections on Human Development*
Max Weber's *The Protestant Ethic and the Spirit of Capitalism*

FEMINISM AND GENDER STUDIES

Judith Butler's *Gender Trouble*
Simone De Beauvoir's *The Second Sex*
Michel Foucault's *History of Sexuality*
Betty Friedan's *The Feminine Mystique*
Saba Mahmood's *The Politics of Piety: The Islamic Revival and the Feminist Subject*
Joan Wallach Scott's *Gender and the Politics of History*
Mary Wollstonecraft's *A Vindication of the Rights of Woman*
Virginia Woolf's *A Room of One's Own*

GEOGRAPHY

The Brundtland Report's *Our Common Future*
Rachel Carson's *Silent Spring*
Charles Darwin's *On the Origin of Species*
James Ferguson's *The Anti-Politics Machine*
Jane Jacobs's *The Death and Life of Great American Cities*
James Lovelock's *Gaia: A New Look at Life on Earth*
Amartya Sen's *Development as Freedom*
Mathis Wackernagel & William Rees's *Our Ecological Footprint*

HISTORY

Janet Abu-Lughod's *Before European Hegemony*
Benedict Anderson's *Imagined Communities*
Bernard Bailyn's *The Ideological Origins of the American Revolution*
Hanna Batatu's *The Old Social Classes And The Revolutionary Movements Of Iraq*
Christopher Browning's *Ordinary Men: Reserve Police Batallion 101 and the Final Solution in Poland*
Edmund Burke's *Reflections on the Revolution in France*
William Cronon's *Nature's Metropolis: Chicago And The Great West*
Alfred W. Crosby's *The Columbian Exchange*
Hamid Dabashi's *Iran: A People Interrupted*
David Brion Davis's *The Problem of Slavery in the Age of Revolution*
Nathalie Zemon Davis's *The Return of Martin Guerre*
Jared Diamond's *Guns, Germs & Steel: the Fate of Human Societies*
Frank Dikotter's *Mao's Great Famine*
John W Dower's *War Without Mercy: Race And Power In The Pacific War*
W. E. B. Du Bois's *The Souls of Black Folk*
Richard J. Evans's *In Defence of History*
Lucien Febvre's *The Problem of Unbelief in the 16th Century*
Sheila Fitzpatrick's *Everyday Stalinism*

Eric Foner's *Reconstruction: America's Unfinished Revolution, 1863-1877*
Michel Foucault's *Discipline and Punish*
Michel Foucault's *History of Sexuality*
Francis Fukuyama's *The End of History and the Last Man*
John Lewis Gaddis's *We Now Know: Rethinking Cold War History*
Ernest Gellner's *Nations and Nationalism*
Eugene Genovese's *Roll, Jordan, Roll: The World the Slaves Made*
Carlo Ginzburg's *The Night Battles*
Daniel Goldhagen's *Hitler's Willing Executioners*
Jack Goldstone's *Revolution and Rebellion in the Early Modern World*
Antonio Gramsci's *The Prison Notebooks*
Alexander Hamilton, John Jay & James Madison's *The Federalist Papers*
Christopher Hill's *The World Turned Upside Down*
Carole Hillenbrand's *The Crusades: Islamic Perspectives*
Thomas Hobbes's *Leviathan*
Eric Hobsbawm's *The Age Of Revolution*
John A. Hobson's *Imperialism: A Study*
Albert Hourani's *History of the Arab Peoples*
Samuel P. Huntington's *The Clash of Civilizations and the Remaking of World Order*
C. L. R. James's *The Black Jacobins*
Tony Judt's *Postwar: A History of Europe Since 1945*
Ernst Kantorowicz's *The King's Two Bodies: A Study in Medieval Political Theology*
Paul Kennedy's *The Rise and Fall of the Great Powers*
Ian Kershaw's *The "Hitler Myth": Image and Reality in the Third Reich*
John Maynard Keynes's *The General Theory of Employment, Interest and Money*
Charles P. Kindleberger's *Manias, Panics and Crashes*
Martin Luther King Jr's *Why We Can't Wait*
Henry Kissinger's *World Order: Reflections on the Character of Nations and the Course of History*
Thomas Kuhn's *The Structure of Scientific Revolutions*
Georges Lefebvre's *The Coming of the French Revolution*
John Locke's *Two Treatises of Government*
Niccolò Machiavelli's *The Prince*
Thomas Robert Malthus's *An Essay on the Principle of Population*
Mahmood Mamdani's *Citizen and Subject: Contemporary Africa And The Legacy Of Late Colonialism*
Karl Marx's *Capital*
Stanley Milgram's *Obedience to Authority*
John Stuart Mill's *On Liberty*
Thomas Paine's *Common Sense*
Thomas Paine's *Rights of Man*
Geoffrey Parker's *Global Crisis: War, Climate Change and Catastrophe in the Seventeenth Century*
Jonathan Riley-Smith's *The First Crusade and the Idea of Crusading*
Jean-Jacques Rousseau's *The Social Contract*
Joan Wallach Scott's *Gender and the Politics of History*
Theda Skocpol's *States and Social Revolutions*
Adam Smith's *The Wealth of Nations*
Timothy Snyder's *Bloodlands: Europe Between Hitler and Stalin*
Sun Tzu's *The Art of War*
Keith Thomas's *Religion and the Decline of Magic*
Thucydides's *The History of the Peloponnesian War*
Frederick Jackson Turner's *The Significance of the Frontier in American History*
Odd Arne Westad's *The Global Cold War: Third World Interventions And The Making Of Our Times*

The Macat Library By Discipline

LITERATURE

Chinua Achebe's *An Image of Africa: Racism in Conrad's Heart of Darkness*
Roland Barthes's *Mythologies*
Homi K. Bhabha's *The Location of Culture*
Judith Butler's *Gender Trouble*
Simone De Beauvoir's *The Second Sex*
Ferdinand De Saussure's *Course in General Linguistics*
T. S. Eliot's *The Sacred Wood: Essays on Poetry and Criticism*
Zora Neale Huston's *Characteristics of Negro Expression*
Toni Morrison's *Playing in the Dark: Whiteness in the American Literary Imagination*
Edward Said's *Orientalism*
Gayatri Chakravorty Spivak's *Can the Subaltern Speak?*
Mary Wollstonecraft's *A Vindication of the Rights of Women*
Virginia Woolf's *A Room of One's Own*

PHILOSOPHY

Elizabeth Anscombe's *Modern Moral Philosophy*
Hannah Arendt's *The Human Condition*
Aristotle's *Metaphysics*
Aristotle's *Nicomachean Ethics*
Edmund Gettier's *Is Justified True Belief Knowledge?*
Georg Wilhelm Friedrich Hegel's *Phenomenology of Spirit*
David Hume's *Dialogues Concerning Natural Religion*
David Hume's *The Enquiry for Human Understanding*
Immanuel Kant's *Religion within the Boundaries of Mere Reason*
Immanuel Kant's *Critique of Pure Reason*
Søren Kierkegaard's *The Sickness Unto Death*
Søren Kierkegaard's *Fear and Trembling*
C. S. Lewis's *The Abolition of Man*
Alasdair MacIntyre's *After Virtue*
Marcus Aurelius's *Meditations*
Friedrich Nietzsche's *On the Genealogy of Morality*
Friedrich Nietzsche's *Beyond Good and Evil*
Plato's *Republic*
Plato's *Symposium*
Jean-Jacques Rousseau's *The Social Contract*
Gilbert Ryle's *The Concept of Mind*
Baruch Spinoza's *Ethics*
Sun Tzu's *The Art of War*
Ludwig Wittgenstein's *Philosophical Investigations*

POLITICS

Benedict Anderson's *Imagined Communities*
Aristotle's *Politics*
Bernard Bailyn's *The Ideological Origins of the American Revolution*
Edmund Burke's *Reflections on the Revolution in France*
John C. Calhoun's *A Disquisition on Government*
Ha-Joon Chang's *Kicking Away the Ladder*
Hamid Dabashi's *Iran: A People Interrupted*
Hamid Dabashi's *Theology of Discontent: The Ideological Foundation of the Islamic Revolution in Iran*
Robert Dahl's *Democracy and its Critics*
Robert Dahl's *Who Governs?*
David Brion Davis's *The Problem of Slavery in the Age of Revolution*

Alexis De Tocqueville's *Democracy in America*
James Ferguson's *The Anti-Politics Machine*
Frank Dikotter's *Mao's Great Famine*
Sheila Fitzpatrick's *Everyday Stalinism*
Eric Foner's *Reconstruction: America's Unfinished Revolution, 1863-1877*
Milton Friedman's *Capitalism and Freedom*
Francis Fukuyama's *The End of History and the Last Man*
John Lewis Gaddis's *We Now Know: Rethinking Cold War History*
Ernest Gellner's *Nations and Nationalism*
David Graeber's *Debt: the First 5000 Years*
Antonio Gramsci's *The Prison Notebooks*
Alexander Hamilton, John Jay & James Madison's *The Federalist Papers*
Friedrich Hayek's *The Road to Serfdom*
Christopher Hill's *The World Turned Upside Down*
Thomas Hobbes's *Leviathan*
John A. Hobson's *Imperialism: A Study*
Samuel P. Huntington's *The Clash of Civilizations and the Remaking of World Order*
Tony Judt's *Postwar: A History of Europe Since 1945*
David C. Kang's *China Rising: Peace, Power and Order in East Asia*
Paul Kennedy's *The Rise and Fall of Great Powers*
Robert Keohane's *After Hegemony*
Martin Luther King Jr.'s *Why We Can't Wait*
Henry Kissinger's *World Order: Reflections on the Character of Nations and the Course of History*
John Locke's *Two Treatises of Government*
Niccolò Machiavelli's *The Prince*
Thomas Robert Malthus's *An Essay on the Principle of Population*
Mahmood Mamdani's *Citizen and Subject: Contemporary Africa And The Legacy Of Late Colonialism*
Karl Marx's *Capital*
John Stuart Mill's *On Liberty*
John Stuart Mill's *Utilitarianism*
Hans Morgenthau's *Politics Among Nations*
Thomas Paine's *Common Sense*
Thomas Paine's *Rights of Man*
Thomas Piketty's *Capital in the Twenty-First Century*
Robert D. Putnam's *Bowling Alone*
John Rawls's *Theory of Justice*
Jean-Jacques Rousseau's *The Social Contract*
Theda Skocpol's *States and Social Revolutions*
Adam Smith's *The Wealth of Nations*
Sun Tzu's *The Art of War*
Henry David Thoreau's *Civil Disobedience*
Thucydides's *The History of the Peloponnesian War*
Kenneth Waltz's *Theory of International Politics*
Max Weber's *Politics as a Vocation*
Odd Arne Westad's *The Global Cold War: Third World Interventions And The Making Of Our Times*

POSTCOLONIAL STUDIES

Roland Barthes's *Mythologies*
Frantz Fanon's *Black Skin, White Masks*
Homi K. Bhabha's *The Location of Culture*
Gustavo Gutiérrez's *A Theology of Liberation*
Edward Said's *Orientalism*
Gayatri Chakravorty Spivak's *Can the Subaltern Speak?*

PSYCHOLOGY

Gordon Allport's *The Nature of Prejudice*
Alan Baddeley & Graham Hitch's *Aggression: A Social Learning Analysis*
Albert Bandura's *Aggression: A Social Learning Analysis*
Leon Festinger's *A Theory of Cognitive Dissonance*
Sigmund Freud's *The Interpretation of Dreams*
Betty Friedan's *The Feminine Mystique*
Michael R. Gottfredson & Travis Hirschi's *A General Theory of Crime*
Eric Hoffer's *The True Believer: Thoughts on the Nature of Mass Movements*
William James's *Principles of Psychology*
Elizabeth Loftus's *Eyewitness Testimony*
A. H. Maslow's *A Theory of Human Motivation*
Stanley Milgram's *Obedience to Authority*
Steven Pinker's *The Better Angels of Our Nature*
Oliver Sacks's *The Man Who Mistook His Wife For a Hat*
Richard Thaler & Cass Sunstein's *Nudge: Improving Decisions About Health, Wealth and Happiness*
Amos Tversky's *Judgment under Uncertainty: Heuristics and Biases*
Philip Zimbardo's *The Lucifer Effect*

SCIENCE

Rachel Carson's *Silent Spring*
William Cronon's *Nature's Metropolis: Chicago And The Great West*
Alfred W. Crosby's *The Columbian Exchange*
Charles Darwin's *On the Origin of Species*
Richard Dawkin's *The Selfish Gene*
Thomas Kuhn's *The Structure of Scientific Revolutions*
Geoffrey Parker's *Global Crisis: War, Climate Change and Catastrophe in the Seventeenth Century*
Mathis Wackernagel & William Rees's *Our Ecological Footprint*

SOCIOLOGY

Michelle Alexander's *The New Jim Crow: Mass Incarceration in the Age of Colorblindness*
Gordon Allport's *The Nature of Prejudice*
Albert Bandura's *Aggression: A Social Learning Analysis*
Hanna Batatu's *The Old Social Classes And The Revolutionary Movements Of Iraq*
Ha-Joon Chang's *Kicking Away the Ladder*
W. E. B. Du Bois's *The Souls of Black Folk*
Émile Durkheim's *On Suicide*
Frantz Fanon's *Black Skin, White Masks*
Frantz Fanon's *The Wretched of the Earth*
Eric Foner's *Reconstruction: America's Unfinished Revolution, 1863-1877*
Eugene Genovese's *Roll, Jordan, Roll: The World the Slaves Made*
Jack Goldstone's *Revolution and Rebellion in the Early Modern World*
Antonio Gramsci's *The Prison Notebooks*
Richard Herrnstein & Charles A Murray's *The Bell Curve: Intelligence and Class Structure in American Life*
Eric Hoffer's *The True Believer: Thoughts on the Nature of Mass Movements*
Jane Jacobs's *The Death and Life of Great American Cities*
Robert Lucas's *Why Doesn't Capital Flow from Rich to Poor Countries?*
Jay Macleod's *Ain't No Makin' It: Aspirations and Attainment in a Low Income Neighborhood*
Elaine May's *Homeward Bound: American Families in the Cold War Era*
Douglas McGregor's *The Human Side of Enterprise*
C. Wright Mills's *The Sociological Imagination*

Thomas Piketty's *Capital in the Twenty-First Century*
Robert D. Putman's *Bowling Alone*
David Riesman's *The Lonely Crowd: A Study of the Changing American Character*
Edward Said's *Orientalism*
Joan Wallach Scott's *Gender and the Politics of History*
Theda Skocpol's *States and Social Revolutions*
Max Weber's *The Protestant Ethic and the Spirit of Capitalism*

THEOLOGY

Augustine's *Confessions*
Benedict's *Rule of St Benedict*
Gustavo Gutiérrez's *A Theology of Liberation*
Carole Hillenbrand's *The Crusades: Islamic Perspectives*
David Hume's *Dialogues Concerning Natural Religion*
Immanuel Kant's *Religion within the Boundaries of Mere Reason*
Ernst Kantorowicz's *The King's Two Bodies: A Study in Medieval Political Theology*
Søren Kierkegaard's *The Sickness Unto Death*
C. S. Lewis's *The Abolition of Man*
Saba Mahmood's *The Politics of Piety: The Islamic Revival and the Feminist Subject*
Baruch Spinoza's *Ethics*
Keith Thomas's *Religion and the Decline of Magic*

COMING SOON

Chris Argyris's *The Individual and the Organisation*
Seyla Benhabib's *The Rights of Others*
Walter Benjamin's *The Work Of Art in the Age of Mechanical Reproduction*
John Berger's *Ways of Seeing*
Pierre Bourdieu's *Outline of a Theory of Practice*
Mary Douglas's *Purity and Danger*
Roland Dworkin's *Taking Rights Seriously*
James G. March's *Exploration and Exploitation in Organisational Learning*
Ikujiro Nonaka's *A Dynamic Theory of Organizational Knowledge Creation*
Griselda Pollock's *Vision and Difference*
Amartya Sen's *Inequality Re-Examined*
Susan Sontag's *On Photography*
Yasser Tabbaa's *The Transformation of Islamic Art*
Ludwig von Mises's *Theory of Money and Credit*

Macat Disciplines

Access the greatest ideas and thinkers
across entire disciplines, including

Postcolonial Studies

Roland Barthes's *Mythologies*
Frantz Fanon's *Black Skin, White Masks*
Homi K. Bhabha's *The Location of Culture*
Gustavo Gutiérrez's *A Theology of Liberation*
Edward Said's *Orientalism*
Gayatri Chakravorty Spivak's *Can the Subaltern Speak?*

 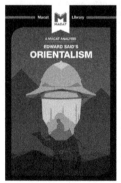 

Macat analyses are available from all good bookshops and libraries.

Access hundreds of analyses through one, multimedia tool.
Join free for one month **library.macat.com**

Macat Disciplines

Access the greatest ideas and thinkers across entire disciplines, including

AFRICANA STUDIES

Chinua Achebe's *An Image of Africa:
Racism in Conrad's Heart of Darkness*

W. E. B. Du Bois's *The Souls of Black Folk*

Zora Neale Hurston's *Characteristics of Negro Expression*

Martin Luther King Jr.'s *Why We Can't Wait*

Toni Morrison's *Playing in the Dark:
Whiteness in the American Literary Imagination*

Macat analyses are available from all good bookshops and libraries.

Access hundreds of analyses through one, multimedia tool.
Join free for one month **library.macat.com**

Macat Disciplines

*Access the greatest ideas and thinkers
across entire disciplines, including*

MACAT

FEMINISM, GENDER AND QUEER STUDIES

Simone De Beauvoir's
The Second Sex

Michel Foucault's
History of Sexuality

Betty Friedan's
The Feminine Mystique

Saba Mahmood's
*The Politics of Piety:
The Islamic Revival and
the Feminist Subject*

Joan Wallach Scott's
*Gender and the
Politics of History*

Mary Wollstonecraft's
*A Vindication of the
Rights of Woman*

Virginia Woolf's
A Room of One's Own

Judith Butler's
Gender Trouble

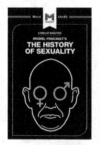

Macat Disciplines

Access the greatest ideas and thinkers across entire disciplines, including

CRIMINOLOGY

Michelle Alexander's
*The New Jim Crow:
Mass Incarceration in the
Age of Colorblindness*

**Michael R. Gottfredson
& Travis Hirschi's**
A General Theory of Crime

Elizabeth Loftus's
Eyewitness Testimony

**Richard Herrnstein
& Charles A. Murray's**
*The Bell Curve: Intelligence and
Class Structure in American Life*

Jay Macleod's
*Ain't No Makin' It:
Aspirations and Attainment in a
Low-Income Neighborhood*

Philip Zimbardo's
The Lucifer Effect

Macat Disciplines

Access the greatest ideas and thinkers across entire disciplines, including

INEQUALITY

Ha-Joon Chang's, *Kicking Away the Ladder*

David Graeber's, *Debt: The First 5000 Years*

Robert E. Lucas's, *Why Doesn't Capital Flow from Rich To Poor Countries?*

Thomas Piketty's, *Capital in the Twenty-First Century*

Amartya Sen's, *Inequality Re-Examined*

Mahbub Ul Haq's, *Reflections on Human Development*

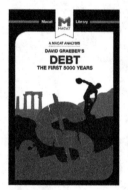

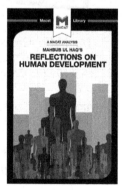

Macat analyses are available from all good bookshops and libraries.

Access hundreds of analyses through one, multimedia tool.
Join free for one month **library.macat.com**

Macat Disciplines

Access the greatest ideas and thinkers across entire disciplines, including

GLOBALIZATION

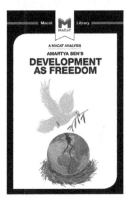

Arjun Appadurai's, *Modernity at Large: Cultural Dimensions of Globalisation*

James Ferguson's, *The Anti-Politics Machine*

Geert Hofstede's, *Culture's Consequences*

Amartya Sen's, *Development as Freedom*

Printed in the United States
by Baker & Taylor Publisher Services